Can you hear
what I see?

HOW WORDS AND ACTIONS MATTER

Library of Congress Control Number: 2014918037
ISBN: 978-0-9908739-0-7

Cover Design: Hitch Design Studio, Brookings, SD

Printed in the United States of America

Life's Great Moments
P.O. Box 742
Brookings, SD 57006

Website www.vj-smith.com

Contents

PART THREE: *CHARACTER*

PART FOUR: *ATTITUDE*

PART FIVE: *CONNECTING*

Introduction: A Gift from Time

My older brother Tim asked Santa Claus to bring him a leprechaun for Christmas. Inspired by the Walt Disney movie *Darby O'Gill and the Little People*, Tim hatched a brilliant plan to own a leprechaun for himself.

The promised pot of gold that accompanied the otherworldly gnome would instantly make my brother the richest second-grader in town. Not dwelling on the value of precious metals, Tim had something else in mind. He knew the magical powers of the Irish fairy and envisioned every day being Christmas Day filled with shiny toys and mounds of succulent candies. Those things would be only one wish away.

Oh, that Tim was a clever one.

Then, my father broke the bad news. Keeping a straight face and acting like a funeral director, he told Tim that Santa Claus would not be going to Ireland that Christmas and wouldn't be able to snare him a leprechaun.

Tim bought it. He was devastated, but he believed the old man. Tears flowing, a dream crushed, he was forced to settle for a railroad train set and a stocking filled with fruit and nuts. It would be another same-old, same-old Christmas. In time, Tim would come to understand the mythical natures of both Santa Claus and leprechauns.

The passage of time allows us the opportunity to gain wisdom. *Opportunity* is the operative word as getting older doesn't necessarily translate into getting smarter. Aging does expose us to more situations where we can continue to learn. It is one of time's gifts, but we can appreciate it only if we care to pay attention.

That is the underlying theme of this book, essentially a collection of opinions and suggestions. Of course, it would be reasonable to ask, "Who is this person dispensing all this advice?"

During the past several years, in my work as a professional speaker, I have traveled a million miles and talked to almost a million people. Many of them have spoken to me after my speeches or have reached out to me in letters – I've received thousands. People have shared their personal stories or thoughts on what is important to them. One of those personal stories became my book, "The Richest Man in Town."

I've listened a lot, and I've learned a lot. My education continued well after college with work, marriage and children. Early on I was a bill collector and then a salesman. I wasn't very good at either job.

For several years I was employed by a manufacturing facility that made non-nuclear components for nuclear weapons – yeah, the big ones. My career path took a sharp and welcome turn when I became an assistant athletic director at my alma mater and then its alumni director. All along the way I was exposed to fascinating experiences and memorable people.

On these pages I share personal observations about things that I think matter – at least to me. I don't claim to have all the answers. I am still learning, too. I want you to take a journey with me and ponder situations, thoughts and ideas – some big, some small and some a little goofy.

PART ONE:

GROWTH

Write Down Your Goals

This *can* change your life. It completely changed mine.

One particular morning I woke up in my bed (it's always good to wake up in your bed) and looked at the ceiling. It was my fortieth birthday and I did not feel like celebrating. My initial thought was, "My life is half over!" As I lay there feeling sorry for myself and watching the ceiling fan going around in endless circles, I wondered if I had been doing the same thing in my life – not really going anywhere, just spinning.

Trying to be positive, I quickly turned my thoughts to what I hoped would be another forty years. What do I want to do with the time I have left? It was the first time some real urgency had crept into my thinking.

For years I'd heard many successful people talk about the importance of setting goals. It sounded good but I'd quickly brush it off by reasoning that I had plenty of time left. Besides, I was too busy living and the whole idea of setting goals would require deep thought, planning and some work. Worse, I feared setting myself up for failure. So, why bother?

Hitting the milestone of forty years changed me. I pushed back on the negative whispers that had found refuge in my brain, sat down at my computer and typed the heading "Goals for My Lifetime." I asked myself two simple questions: What do you want to do? Can you do it before you die?

For two hours I reflected and pecked away on the keyboard. I thought about places I'd read about or seen on television that I wanted to visit. I thought about the perfect job that matched my interests with my skills. I thought about charitable causes and how I might help. I thought about a modest legacy to prove that I was here. And, I thought about my deceased parents and if they would be proud to call me their son.

When finished, I'd typed fifty-seven goals. Some big, some small – each one was important to me. I printed out the list and began studying it. It dawned on me that I was holding a blueprint for the rest of my life. I was looking at my future. That is, my future if I got focused and did the work.

Sure, it was a little daunting to look at the list. Where do I begin? The answer was to pick one goal and do it.

That's how I found myself at the University of

Notre Dame watching the Irish play the Northwestern Wildcats in a football game. One of the goals I had written was to see a football game at that legendary place. There were moments during that football contest that I marveled that I was even there. A second thought was, "One goal down, fifty-six to go."

Early on, I realized that hope wasn't a good strategy in trying to make these things happen. The difference between hoping to achieve goals and actually achieving them boiled down to focus and the amount of effort I was going to give. Nothing was going to fall into my lap. If I wanted something, I had to go and get it.

Plus, I came to understand that I had to give either my time or my money to achieve my goals. That is an important thing to consider. There is a cost and you need to be prepared to pay it.

To date, I've accomplished forty-four of the goals I wrote down when I turned forty. (This book is a product of that list.) I've taken a hot-air balloon ride, gone salmon fishing on the Kenai River in Alaska, planted a tree, watched the swallows at Mission San Juan Capistrano, gazed at Michelangelo's masterpiece which adorns the ceiling of the Sistine Chapel in Rome and stood at the base of General Sherman in Sequoia

National Park, the largest tree on Earth. Honestly, I probably wouldn't have done any of those without that list.

Have I had any failures? One goal was to win a trophy at Toastmasters Internationals' Worlds Championship of Public Speaking. I tried but failed. On two occasions I made it to the contest finals but came up short. No first place, no second place and no third place – no hardware. I wasn't good enough, but it hurt not to win anything. After getting past the sting of defeat I realized I got what I truly wanted all along and that was to get better at public speaking.

Sometimes in the fog of failing to achieve a goal you can lose sight of a small victory. Trying brings its own sense of success.

Nudging me along in my life's journey are those goals I wrote down. That simple act has given me focus and reminds me that it's not about the things to do before you die. Rather, it's about the things to do to make for a meaningful, interesting and active life.

Take that step and you will be amazed by the future you can create.

Develop a Sixth Sense of Awareness

As I thought about the topic of awareness, I typed into my computer's search engine: "the gift of awareness." What I got back were pages upon pages of self-oriented articles on how people can be more aware of their inner needs. Not diminishing the importance of discovering what people desire for self-fulfillment, I was surprised that I couldn't find anything about being more aware of the needs of the people we encounter during our daily routines.

Special people possess a sixth sense. It's hard to define, but you know it when you see it. These individuals are keenly aware of what is happening around them, fully mindful of how their behavior affects others and constantly anticipating situations. They are always one step ahead of everyone else. They hold open doors for you when your hands are full, step aside when you need to get around them, come to your assistance without being asked, and take care of details you never would have thought about. They are always thinking – calculating how they may help other people, even if just for a moment. Their behavior is invaluable.

But, alas, so many people are singularly focused. They see what is directly in front of them but are oblivious as to what is going on around them. They don't understand how their action or lack of action impacts other people. For them, little time is spent anticipating their next move and what might or might not happen. You can forget about them looking out for other people as they are focused on their needs alone.

I don't dismiss these individuals as uncaring, just unaware. They don't spend much time thinking about such things. It's not how their brains work.

That's why aware people hold such a special place. Armed with great observation skills, a smile and chock-full of good manners, they are wholly in tune with the present. They are always paying attention and doing little things to brighten our day.

They are some of my favorites.

A Book or a Class Doesn't Make You an Expert

On the eve of one of my speaking engagements, I attended a social gathering consisting of some people who would be in the audience the following morning. A young man asked me what I was going to talk about. Just as I started to answer his question, I was interrupted by a sixty-something-year-old woman who said, "I had a speech class when I was in college and I can offer you some tips."

Her comment caught me off-guard. Up to that point I'd logged more than 2,000 speaking appearances all over the country. I figured my personal experiences trumped her long-ago college class and I told her as much.

She simply shrugged her shoulders and walked away. It was obvious she was disappointed that she was not able to impart some of her wisdom on me. In hindsight, I probably should have listened to her, smiled and politely thanked her for her input.

Likewise, I've met people who have read one book on a particular subject and declared themselves resident experts. I'm reminded of a poignant comment written by a young man who read historian David McCullough's Pulitzer Prize winning book, *Truman*. McCullough's epic biography of Harry Truman is over a thousand pages in length and is bursting with information on our thirty-third president.

To which the young man wrote: "For about two

months I was a Harry Truman expert. Then I forgot almost everything."

Therein is the difference between living something versus merely learning about it. When you live it – to experience it fully – it becomes a part of who you are. On the other hand, if you are exposed to something only in a classroom setting or in a book, much is quickly forgotten.

So to my point, experience is the best teacher in life. There is no substitute for it. Experience is fiercely honest in assessing abilities and shows no favoritism. And, to win her favor, a person must be vigilant in not repeating mistakes from previous lessons, lest they be reminded of their shortcomings once again. She can be cruel but she is fair.

I fully appreciate the qualities of enthusiasm and having a positive attitude. Yet, it was only through my *experiences* that I came to understand the importance of those attributes. Thus, experience is the mother of all learning.

Recent graduates find it difficult to get a coveted first job because they are generally competing with people who have prior experience. "How can I get experience if nobody gives me a job?" the frustrated graduate asks. It doesn't seem fair at the time but once the experience is gained, the lesson is understood – experience matters. And, the once-shunned applicant becomes an advocate for experience, too.

Just one more comment on this subject. During my working career I met several freshly minted college graduates who showed up on the first day of the job with chips on their shoulders and believing they had all the answers. The arrogant new hires were quickly shunned by the veteran members of the group. And, until they showed a little humility and a desire to work as a member of a team, they remained isolated.

Some figured it out and some never did.

Be Cautious of What You Read

There is an intriguing story out there about the American buffalo. The writer, believing we can learn a valuable lesson from the earliest prairie cow, extolled the virtues of the great beast when facing adversity.

He stated that a buffalo will run directly into the path of an oncoming thunderstorm. Why? It was his contention that the buffalo knows that by running into threatening weather it will pass quicker. Rather than standing around and enduring the full wrath of a storm, the wise buffalo has opted to take action – meeting the challenge head-on, thus getting past the problem sooner so it can get back to important business of eating grass.

Not able to talk to a buffalo, but wanting to know the validity of the author's claims, I called a guy who had worked with buffalo for more than thirty years. After explaining what I read, I asked the buffalo expert what he thought. He replied, "Makes for a nice story, doesn't it?" In all of his years of being around buffalo, he had never noted this trait.

We like nice stories. More to the point, we like and believe stories that appeal to our values, interests, political persuasions and spiritual leanings. Other stuff is suspect.

When asked, the vast majority of people will say, "Don't believe everything you read on the Internet." Yet, many of those same individuals will repeat something gleaned online because it supports their ideas.

I'm reminded of the time I was driving down a lonely stretch of highway and listening to a talk radio program. The program host, wanting listeners to join him in his hostility toward members of the United

States Congress, read a laundry list of criminal activity supposedly perpetrated by the elected officials. It was quite damning and included: twenty-nine members arrested for spousal abuse; eighty-four got caught driving drunk; nineteen found to have written bad checks; eight arrested for shoplifting; and fourteen were collared on drug related charges.

Who elected those bums?

Conveniently, no names were given, just numbers. Then the host revealed his source for the information: the Internet. That made me mad so I grabbed my cell phone and called the radio station and asked to speak to the man behind the microphone. To my surprise, the secretary immediately transferred me to the guy and we were live on air.

Not backing down, I told the host that he was doing a disservice by passing along information taken from an unreliable source. Further, I said I wasn't being a cheerleader for the United States Congress but I didn't need lies or scurrilous accusations to support my opinion. Finally, I told him his listeners trusted him and he had the responsibility to check his information for accuracy before he broadcast it.

Click. He hung up on me. People in charge of microphones have the power to do those things.

We live in the Information Age. Anyone with a keyboard and an axe to grind has a platform to try to be whatever he or she wants to be. Bloggers and social media engineers have an undying need to stay relevant. They do so by making varying degrees of provocative statements, thus stirring emotions in the reader. To which, more banter yields more readers; more readers yields more dollars from advertisers; more dollars from advertisers yields happy bosses; and, happy bosses keep the writers employed. It's a nice tight circle.

Stepping back from all of this, the reader needs to ask a simple question: What is the writer's purpose? Disguised within carefully proportioned pieces of selected information, most writers are looking to lead the reader to a certain conclusion – theirs. The heck with objectivity; just see it my way. Thus, the primary intent is not to inform but to persuade.

The best vaccine to guard against ignorance or being led astray is to read as much as you can from a variety of sources. That's right, read. Stay inquisitive and constantly seek the truth. If something you've heard or read doesn't sound quite right, well, it probably isn't.

Question everything. Don't just accept

everything you read or hear.

Never stop learning no matter your age. Not long ago I visited my wife's grandmother at a long-term care facility. When I entered her room I noticed she had her face very close to the loud television and she was fully focused on what she was watching. I shouted, "What are you doing?" She looked up at me and said, "I'm watching Fox News to see what the Republicans are thinking. In a little while I'll turn it over to CNN to see what the Democrats are thinking."

My wife's grandmother is one hundred three years old.

Thomas Jefferson, author of the Declaration of Independence, the third President of the United States and one of the four guys on Mount Rushmore, wrote this: "The cornerstone of democracy rests on the foundation of an educated electorate." In other words, the voters need to have a clue about what or who they are voting for.

Voting might be a right, but being an informed voter is a duty. A lot is riding on it.

Practice the Art of Listening

I had just finished speaking to an audience of senior citizens when a man approached me eager to share a story about his grandson. Just a month prior, he was babysitting the five-year-old in the basement of his home. The two of them were on a couch. Grandpa had the television on, trying to watch a news program. The grandson, doing what young boys do, was jumping up and down on the couch and spewing forth a long, never-ending sentence. Children talk like that.

Every so often the grandfather would nod his head and grunt. This was his attempt to make the child think he was actually paying attention. Not fooled, the youngster wrapped his hands around his grandfather's head and turned it toward him. Then, staring face to face, the grandson said, "Grandpa, I want you to listen to me with your eyes!"

Even kids can figure it out. When you look into someone's eyes you are telling him that he is important, he matters, he counts.

This lesson was galvanized in my head by a young man who happened to be a teacher. He told me he had a mild form of autism and his brain wouldn't let him look directly into the eyes of other people. Surprised to hear this, I said, "But you are looking into my eyes right now."

He smiled and said, "No I'm not. I'm looking at the bridge of your nose."

That moment brought chills to my spine and still does. Here was a young man, a teacher, struggling with a disability yet understanding the powerful message sent by looking into another human being's eyes. I hugged the guy and thanked him for sharing his story.

Unfortunately, I've met so many people in my life who while I'm talking to them, constantly survey the landscape – looking for whomever or whatever. It seems like their heads are on a swivel. You feel like grabbing them and saying, "Hey, I'm right here!"

On the other hand, I may just be an extremely boring guy and they don't want to talk to me.

Over the years I've been told by "experts" that in some cultures it is considered an insult to look into another person's eyes. Specifically, they mention Native Americans, Asians and people from the Middle East. Well, I have talked to hundreds of people from those cultural backgrounds and not one person has told me this. Nor, during our conversations, have they avoided eye contact with me. My personal jury is still out on that deal.

On this topic, I think Mr. Miyagi said it best. He was the wise old karate instructor from the movie, *The Karate Kid*. He told his pupil Daniel son, "Look eye! Always look eye!"

Yes, it sends a powerful message.

Give Yourself Something to Look Forward To

I love Thelma's attitude.

I've known her since I was a little kid. I would secretly climb her apple trees and steal the coveted fruit. As I have discovered, my methods weren't as stealthy as I thought. She knew all the apple thieves in the neighborhood.

Every few weeks I see her at the grocery store. During our brief conversations, she rattles off all the things she needs to do during the upcoming week. She doesn't do this to impress me; rather, it's her way of saying, "This needs to be quick because I've got things to do."

And, boy, does she ever. Thelma is an active member of more than half a dozen service organizations. If she isn't baking a cake or cookies for a funeral, then she's at a nursing home or a hospital visiting the sick. Her calendar is full. Even at the age of eighty-five, she spent three bone-chilling February days at our Capitol lobbying legislators on behalf of military veterans.

She lost her husband, Albert, in 2004. Two years later, Thelma had heart bypass surgery and spent four days in a coma. After that, she tells me, "I vowed to make every minute count."

In return for all her volunteer efforts, Thelma is rewarded with something that is hard to describe but brings incredible value to her life – a sense of self-worth. "Visiting the sick makes me feel better," she says, "because I help other people feel better."

Thelma is a doer. In the process of doing, "I make new friends and new discoveries all the time," she says. That quest for discovery brings freshness to her life. She gets out of bed each morning excited about her day.

Thelma shares a common bond with my friend Chuck. He's eighty-one and has written twenty books.

Twenty! Most people, rightly, would feel great about writing one book. The amazing thing is that each of his twenty books was published *after* he turned sixty-five. And, Chuck is always looking for ideas on another book.

Chuck has had his health scares, too. "I do wonder sometimes about my luck about living so long, although I've been through bladder cancer and five bypasses so I'm not really dreading whatever comes next," he said.

His self-motivation comes in the form of lists. Each evening he makes a list of things he wants to accomplish the next day. The lists give him focus. Making little checkmarks after completing tasks, both big and small, brings quiet satisfaction that his life has purpose – he's getting stuff done.

Both Chuck and Thelma have added real zest to their years; they always have something to look forward to. They are fun to be around as there is excitement in their voices. After talking to them you are inspired to do more.

Having something to look forward to is not the exclusive territory of the senior generation. On the contrary, it's best to begin thinking this way early in life lest you want to join the old chorus of "I wished I would've" or "I really should've."

It doesn't have to be big stuff, either. Lots of little things add up to big things. How about some of these: Call a friend you haven't talked to in years. Take a child or an elderly friend out to lunch. Clean out your closet. Volunteer at a soup kitchen. Visit a zoo. Plant a tree. Look at a map and think about new places to go (you don't have to actually go, but it is fun to think about). Commit yourself to reading that book that you've always wanted to read. Write a letter to someone who has made a difference in your life, telling him or her just what it's meant to you, and have the courage to send it. Join a group that benefits children. Start a hobby. Begin writing a personal history about your life; you might not think it's a big deal, but it will be a treasure to your loved ones.

Dang it, try to do something!

I used to work with a guy named Ted. Each day he would come to work and announce the number of days left before he retired. He'd say, "I've got 267 more giddy-ups!" The smile on his face grew larger as his final work day drew nearer. On his last day he said, "This is it boys! You all can cry when I'm sitting in my chair doing nothing."

Just two months after his last giddy-up, Ted

died.

As I've grown older, I've thought a lot about Ted and his seemingly singular focus. Sadly, I don't remember anything else about him; the only thing he wanted to talk about was retiring. I understood his looking forward to retirement, but wonder if once he got there he asked himself, "Now what?"

Granted, the idea of having something to look forward to may produce its share of disappointments. When I was in the fifth grade, my teacher told the class about Halley's Comet. The long-tailed gigantic space ice-ball was last seen by Earthlings in 1910 and it would make its next visit in 1986. What luck! That meant we would be able to witness a celestial event that had made generations of dumbstruck people fall to their knees and beg for God's mercy.

It was a cosmic dud. The danged thing showed up on the other side of the solar system.

Some things are out of our control. Yet, there is so much that we can control if we have the guts and gumption to take action.   Why would we allow our destinies to be shaped by relinquishing the steering wheel of our lives to an unknown force taking us to a place we may not want to go? Why would we do that?

Take a lesson from Thelma and Chuck. Don't

just exist – have something to look forward to and go do it. We don't know the number of days we get, but we are in charge of what we put in them. And, I'm convinced we add years to our life by putting life in our years.

Get going.

Never Write in Anger

It's really stupid to do this.

Let me add a point of clarification. You can write an angry letter, text or email – just don't send it. Heck, the whole process can be good for you. Unleashing pent-up frustrations and pushing past the boundaries of civil communication – getting something off your chest and using colorful language to boot – can be great therapy and you don't have to pay for it.

I've written lots of "you ignorant jerk" letters and emails. Every single one of them ended up in the wastebasket or trash folder. None got sent.

Why? Simply, I knew I would be the biggest loser. Those angry outbursts would have had the direct opposite impacts of what I'd intended. Worse, the recipients of the notes would have had tangible proof that I was the problem. Nothing would have been accomplished other than selfish pot-stirring on my part. So, what's the point?

Today's ubiquitous forums for electronic communication have afforded people the opportunity to attain instant idiot status for the whole world to witness. It's amazing how many texts, postings and tweets are sent in a cloud of anger. The senders come off as hot heads or cry babies – neither one an endearing title. Then, the offending individuals are forced to retreat and hopefully apologize. Unfortunately, some never learn and go back to being stupid again.

What are these people thinking? That's the problem – they aren't.

Abraham Lincoln was perhaps the wisest of our chief executives. His secretary of war, Edwin Stanton, was a man of great ego who was never to be challenged. An Army officer accused Stanton of favoritism and the cabinet secretary was livid. Lincoln told the angry Stanton to write a letter to the officer but not send it until he could review it.

Impressed with the brilliant cutting words of his freshly completed letter, Stanton proudly presented it for inspection. Lincoln read the letter and said, "Put it in the stove." Stanton protested. Lincoln continued, "That's what I do when I have written a letter when I'm angry. It's a good letter and you had a good time writing it and you feel better. Now burn it and write another."

That's wisdom.

Always Send a Note of Thanks

I'm shocked by the number of people who don't send thank you notes. Whenever I speak on the topic of gratitude, I ask the members of the audience, "How many of you are still waiting for a thank you card for a gift you've given in the past year?" Invariably, half the people will raise a hand.

Half! That's a lot of people waiting to be thanked. And, don't think they will conveniently forget about it, either.

I urge people to send thank you notes the old fashioned way – written by hand and delivered via the United States Postal Service. Some individuals have told me that I need to "get with the times" and accept computer-driven notes of thanks. No thank you. If the intent of a note of thanks is to demonstrate sincere gratitude, using the simplest and easiest way to do it doesn't seem to send the right message. Besides, to read a person's heartfelt penned words is priceless and there is no substitute for it. Many people will read a thank you note two to three times. It makes them feel good and rightfully so.

After I spoke at a conference a few years ago, a woman approached me and asked to talk to me in private. We walked over to a quiet corner and I asked her what was on her mind. She told me that she had been married for five years. Then she added, "I never sent thank you cards for the gifts I received. I started feeling guilty when you talked about it. What do you think I should do?"

Without hesitating, I said, "I think I'd get busy and start writing thank you notes." She felt uncomfortable with my answer. "But don't you think most of those people will have forgotten? If I send them now I will look either lazy or ungrateful."

She had a point, but I wasn't about to back down. "During my speech, when I asked the question about who was waiting for a thank you card for a gift you've given in the past year, did you raise your hand?" The look of stubbornness left her face as guilt set in.

"Yeah, I raised my hand. My niece hasn't thanked me for the fifty dollars I gave her for a graduation gift. That was almost a year ago."

"I think you've answered your own question," I said.

Yes, people remember and most gift givers expect a note of thanks from the person who receives their gift. Taking time to send appreciative words is a show of good manners. And, at its most basic, it's an acknowledgment that a gift has been received. So often, gift givers are left to wonder if their wedding, birthday or holiday present ever made it to their intended destination.

The individual who doesn't send thank you notes comes across as selfish and gives the appearance of thinking, "It's all about me." Conversely, the person who takes the time to write thank you notes enhances his or her image. Gift givers think even more highly of the recipients.

This leads me to one of the great stories shared with me during my travels. I had just finished speaking at a convention and a tall man with a big grin walked up to me and said, "I have a story for you!"

Lots of people tell me stories and I appreciate hearing all of them. Yet, only a few stick with me. This one I will take to my grave.

The man said he was a financial planner and he had an older female client who just happened to be a millionaire. The woman had four grandsons and every year on their birthdays she would send each one a hundred dollars. Three of the four grandsons always sent her thank you notes. One grandson never sent anything.

"Here's the deal," the financial planner told me. "My client died eighteen months ago. She left three of the grandsons a million dollars each. The fourth grandson got a letter from his grandmother explaining that because he never sent her a thank you card he would get nothing. All she wanted was to feel appreciated."

It was an expensive lesson.

Something Extra:
It's Easier to Tear Down Than to Build Up

A once-grand building that may have taken years to plan and erect can be knocked down in a carefully planned, dynamite-filled instant. Getting past the excitement of the flashes of light, the choreographed explosions and the rolling clouds of dust, it's always a reflective moment for me.

Perhaps an architect's dream project or a construction company's proudest accomplishment is reduced to useless rubble at the push of a button. It takes far less time to destroy than it does to build.

Likewise, it's been my observation that some people operate the same way. Fueled by envy or other motives, they say hurtful things, spread rumors and tell outright lies with the intended purpose of tearing down other individuals to their "woe is me" level. Rather than doing what it takes to attain a certain level of success or achievement for themselves, they choose an easier path – and let their acid tongues do the dirty work. They want to level the playing field.

Oh, the ugly sin of jealousy. It's a destructive force that prevents some people from dealing with reality. Part of that reality is that some family members, neighbors, co-workers or acquaintances are going to have things *they* want. Those coveted items might include fame, fortune, a job promotion, a new car or new home.

My experience is that there will always be people with more stuff. And, there will always be people with less stuff. That is the law of stuff. And, frankly, it's just stuff.

Jealousy is an emotional response brought on by insecurity. For some people, there is a false perception that stuff is directly proportional to one's value. The thought of being perceived as inferior prompts anger, thus lashing out in jealousy. The only remedy for this affliction is to change one's thinking, and that isn't easy.

I don't pretend to be a mental health professional but I believe the first step is to accept the law of stuff because it represents reality.

The second step is to take an inventory of one's sense of self-worth. Putting it a simpler way, to count one's blessings and be truly grateful for all things we have both big and small – primary of which is the gift of life. Honestly, it's a miracle that we are even here. Start with that and everything else falls into place.

Make a personal vow to refrain from making provocative comments whenever there is an urge to speak in a jealous manner. That takes some real discipline. But, a whole new world reveals itself when we get past the stuff and fully appreciate our blessings.

If you need to, start counting.

We do not see things as they are.
We see them as we are.

–The Talmud

PART TWO:

WORK

Be on Time for Everything

When I entered the workforce, I was surrounded by the men and women of the World War II generation. If they arrived for work a few minutes before starting time, they would apologize for running late – even though they weren't late. Things have changed.

It's not just about being on time for work. It spills over into being punctual for meetings, church, job assignments, car-pooling and just about everything else.

This is one of my great pet peeves. I don't understand why some people are always late. Some so-called behavioral experts claim it is a matter of low self-esteem. That's a bunch of bunk. "Low self-esteem" is offered as an excuse for so many human shortfalls.

Being late is a bad habit. As with other bad habits, it comes down to a matter of self-control. If a person dismisses his or her chronic tardiness with a simple, "Well, that's just the way I am," attitude, he or she will suffer the consequences – none of them positive.

Simply stated, not *caring* about being late is

rude and it borders on selfishness. Being late is one thing but not caring about being late brings it into an entirely different realm.

Other people are affected by this behavior. We've all had to patiently wait for these time bandits and then put on a fake happy face when they finally show up. *BREAKING NEWS–* we aren't happy!

Some actually wonder why they never get promoted. They are lucky to keep the jobs they have. As for relationships, I wonder how many arguments happen every day because someone is late. Early in a relationship, the "sorry I'm late" line might be cute, but in time it rubs thin and then it finally rubs raw.

Let's get to another sore spot – starting meetings on time. For years I've watched typical company meetings play out in the same manner. A few people would show up five minutes prior to the appointed meeting hour. The bulk of the people would arrive at the scheduled time. Then, over the next five to ten minutes, others would drift into the meeting. When everyone was assembled, the person who called the meeting would say, "I guess everyone is here so we will begin."

That's positive reinforcement of negative behavior. The person calling the meeting has insulted those who arrived early or right on time. Whether they realize it or not, they have implied that the time of the late people is more valuable than the time of those who arrived early. Worst of all, they have unwittingly told the late people that it's okay to be late. Well, it *isn't* okay to be late without a good excuse.

Just a final thought on the time issue. Few individuals, even the habitually tardy ones, are ever late for an airplane trip. Why? They know the plane will leave without them. No excuses and no dallying around – it then becomes a *priority* to be on time.

In the end, it always comes down to priorities – doesn't it?

A Little Hustle Sends a Big Message

People who hustle win my heart.

It makes up for a lot of mistakes. The best part is it doesn't take any special ability to hustle – so practically anyone can do it, and anywhere. When a person hustles, it's a quiet but potent statement about attitude. And, if they hustle for you, it makes you feel appreciated. Everyone likes to feel appreciated.

Hustling it isn't about running. Rather, it is a noticeable increase in movement with an obvious purpose. You can see it.

Just recently I was at a big box store buying a bag of cat litter. As I lifted the heavy bag out of my shopping cart I accidentally ripped it open and gray cat litter went flying everywhere. The clerk said, "Do you still want that?" I told her I did but that I needed some tape.

The clerk looked at me and asked, "Tape?" I told her I'd tape over the tear in the bag. Still a bit confused, the clerk shouted to the clerk in the next aisle, "Hey Jane, do we have some tape?" The question seemed to stun Jane, too, as she said, "Tape? I don't know. I'll ask Thad."

Thad, as I quickly discovered, was a young manager trainee. It's been my experience that newly appointed manager trainees like to stand around and try to look important. That's the first lesson they try to learn.

Jane called out, "Hey Thad, we need some tape on aisle 12. " Acting as if the request was an unwanted intrusion, Thad replied, "*And just where* am I supposed to find tape?"

At that moment I'm thinking, "We come *here*

to buy tape! You got a thousand rolls on your shelves back there so just grab one!"

Jane directed him to the customer service desk. It soon became apparent that Thad did not approve of an underling telling him what to do so he walked very slowly toward the customer service desk. After securing the tape, Thad started the trek to aisle 12. I didn't think he could get any slower, but he found a lower gear.

It was obvious he was trying to send us a message about his self-importance. So much so that Jane looked at me and said, "Boy, I don't know what *his* problem is."

Jane's comment lit my fire so I bee-lined it toward Thad and intercepted him about fifty feet from aisle 12. I said, "Thad, can I have that tape?" He shrugged his shoulders and handed it to me. Not wanting the teachable moment to pass, I said, "Thad, let me give you a piece of advice. You won't last long at this job or any job if you don't learn how to hustle. Hustle, Thad, hustle!"

To his credit, Thad held his silence, but he wasn't happy. One day, I hope, he will get past his anger toward me and come to understand that a little bit of hustle sends a mighty message.

I wish I could introduce Thad to Mark. Mark is a full-bodied, late-thirties front-line clerk at an upscale taco joint in Phoenix. When I saw Mark for the first time he was sweating profusely.

I'd just stepped inside the taco shop and joined a line of a dozen customers. My first inclination was to go someplace else as it looked like a long wait. Yet, I couldn't take my eyes off Mark because he was in constant motion. And, given his size, it was a lot of motion.

Within a few minutes I realized there were only three people working in the restaurant – Mark at the counter and two ladies in the kitchen. Quickly turning from the cash register after taking an order, Mark would grab a tray full of hot food that just came out of the kitchen, and he would dash to a table to deliver the order. Then, he would bolt back to the cash register to begin the cycle all over again.

Before taking the next order, he would reach down and grab the bottom half of his green apron and wipe the sweat that was streaming from his forehead. Trying to gain a little composure, Mark would then say, "I'm sorry about the wait. What can I get you?"

Every person standing in line realized Mark was moving as fast as he possibly could go. Add in his apology for the delay and Mark had earned our complete devotion. The customers felt sorry for him knowing the restaurant was short-staffed so some of them even pitched in to help. I'm dead serious. One lady bused tables and another woman went around and picked up the little order number placards and returned them to the cash register. A guy filled the napkin dispenser. To each good deed doer, Mark would say, "Thank you. I appreciate it."

When Mark delivered the food to our table he accidentally knocked over my beverage and half of it spilled out on the table. Looking defeated, he immediately said, "I'm so sorry." Frankly, I didn't care. I patted Mark on his shoulder and told him it was okay and that I appreciated his hustle.

There were fifty people in the restaurant. Every one of us knew that Mark was doing the best he could with what he had. That's the most you can expect of anyone.

I respect and admire people who work hard. They are not only remembered but oftentimes rewarded.

That was on full display to me when I flew into Dallas not long ago. The shuttle bus driver for the rental car company was a fifty-year-old superman.

Perhaps fifteen of us were standing at the curb when his bus pulled up. The door flew open and he hopped out in a flash. "Welcome to Dallas!" he shouted with a big smile on his face. If someone would reach down to pick up their bag, he'd say, "Hey, I got it." Then, he would run onto the bus, stow the bag and return for more. No one got on his bus carrying their own bags.

After we got to the rental car lot he said, "It will be lot easier and a lot quicker if I get your bags." All of us got off the bus and watched as he ran in and out of the bus, grabbing our bags and suitcases, and gently placing them on the ground. He completed his chores in less than a minute.

It was at that moment I saw something special. Every passenger gave him a tip. Several of the group, having witnessed the bus driver's extra efforts, reached back into their wallets for more money – a dollar tip became a two-dollar tip and a two-dollar tip became a five-dollar tip.

That bus driver had life figured out. He knew if he gave a little, he would get a little back. If he gave a lot, he would get a lot back. He chose the latter. I've been on dozens of shuttle buses at airports throughout the country. That bus driver in Dallas is the only one I remember.

Mark, the big guy at taco joint in Phoenix, I remember him, too, because he chose to make his customers feel important by moving as fast as he could.

Oh, I remember Thad, the manager trainee, but in a very different way.

The Magic of the Extra Step

It's the signature mark that separates exceptional workers from average workers. Taking an extra step requires a little more effort and a good attitude, but those who have the courage to do it get even more in return.

There's that old adage about going "the extra mile." For many people, a mile seems like a long way. On the other hand, a step is quite doable. Anyone can do a step – if they want to.

In my book *The Richest Man in Town*, I detailed the life of a lovable little guy named Marty. He ran a cash register at our local Wal-Mart store. Customers flocked to his checkout line because he made them feel appreciated. Marty accomplished that by virtue of a simple gesture. Instead of handing back a customer's change and receipt in the usual manner, he did something completely different. He walked around the counter, extended his hand in friendship and sincerely thanked them for their purchase.

It was a moment that created a legacy. Ten years after Marty's death, the people in my hometown remember him with fondness and admiration. He made a difference in an unexpected place.

The same goes for Mike Herr, a United States Post Office clerk at Penn State University. He's affectionately referred to as "Mike the Mailman." Mike's been handing out compliments and bringing joy to postal customers at that location since 1978. His impact is so profound that it attracted the attention of "CBS Evening News" and they featured him in their "On the Road" series.

After viewing that nationally televised segment, I sent Mike a letter and a copy of my book. I shared with him that his story reminded me of Marty's and congratulated him for making a difference in peoples' lives. True to his nature, Mike wrote back to me and included his phone number if I cared to call him. I jumped at the chance.

During our conversation I heard the same significant themes. Mike loves the people who come into the post office and they return the affection. He delights in bringing smiles to the faces of those who stand in his line. Mike feels so lucky to have his job and can't imagine doing anything else. Yet even with all the fame he has attained (he didn't mention this; I found many articles written about him) there was an incredible sense of humility in his voice. I didn't want our conversation to end as I felt I was talking to an old friend.

Even though they never met, Marty and Mike were kindred spirits. By doing a little more – taking the extra step – they have made people feel special. In return, they enriched their own lives. It is a beautiful thing to witness and a reminder of what can happen when we take a moment to lift up the lives of other people.

Marty and Mike figured it out – you get what you give.

Your Work Ethic is Your Calling Card

The best piece of advice I ever heard on work is this: Do what you are supposed to do, when you are supposed to do it by, whether you want to or not.

I wish those words had been etched in my brain when I was a young man. It took me awhile to figure it out. But that simple statement speaks volumes for job security and advancement. Based on that wisdom, if I were to stand in front of a group of young people entering the workforce, I would say the following:

"You must have *discipline* and place a priority on getting to work on time and finishing projects on time. There must be an emphasis on *quality* in everything you do. Things have to be done right. The expression, 'That's good enough' might not be good enough. If it isn't right, go back and do it again – before you are told. Finally, you need to take *responsibility* for your work. Don't pass the buck when something is wrong or you will look weak and maybe a little selfish, too. Own the situation. In the end, your name is attached to it. What does your name mean to you?"

Having personal discipline, doing high-quality work and taking responsibility for one's actions are the three key components for a sound work ethic. And, it's like a three-legged stool. Remove one leg and the stool cannot remain upright. Each must be present.

I've long admired people who demonstrate a positive work ethic. Rather than constantly looking for shortcuts, they take the time to do things the right way, regardless of the extra work it requires. They understand that you never have to apologize when you do things right.

Plus, and this is big, those individuals set an example for others to follow. In time, they usually become leaders within businesses and organizations. Their actions set them apart.

A critical component in all of this spills over into the family. Parents who demonstrate a positive attitude about the importance of work are sending a message to their children – the next generation of workers. Conversely, if a parent constantly complains about his or her job or makes it a habit of calling in sick when he or she isn't sick, well, good luck with the offspring. They will most likely become mirror images of the parent.

I used to work with a guy who had a sign at his desk that proudly proclaimed, "Work Smarter, Not Harder." Yes, common sense tells us to be smarter in our jobs – improve our time management, becoming more efficient and always looking for better ways to do things – all good stuff. As for not working harder, I've never met anyone in my life who got fired for working too hard. On the contrary, the most respected co-workers I have known are those who always tried to do a little more, which of course, required a little more work. They are the ones who got the promotions, too.

The old adage "It all pays the same" might be true, but the dividends are quite different.

Some Jobs Give You Focus

Money is far more prized when it is earned and not just given. That's one reason older people take what seems like an odd sense of pride in having worked hard in their youth and gotten paid very little. While they appreciated having a job – any job – because it sustained them, that early work taught them the value of a job and served as a foundation for future employment.

First jobs are often hard, somewhat monotonous and not a lot of fun. Yet they can put perspective in your head and fire in your belly. They give you an appreciation for the millions of people who do that kind of work every day to survive. And they highlight the importance of getting an education or learning a trade to avoid that kind of work in the future. Plus, there's the enormous sense of satisfaction with getting a paycheck.

It's not an exaggeration to say that my first job out of college challenged my soul. I was hired by a company that financed furniture purchases in Denver. When people failed to pay their monthly installments, I stepped in. The last resort was the dreaded repossession of their furniture.

Within a few days of my new employment, I did my first repo job. I called a man who hadn't paid his bill in several months and during our tense conversation he told me there was no way he could pay as his wife left him. He said, "Just pick up the damned furniture."

So one brisk October night I showed up at his door. He greeted me coldly and introduced me to his fifteen-and sixteen-year-old sons. There was a look of hate in their eyes and I understood why. Then, the man led me to a bedroom and pointed to the unpaid furniture. One of the items happened to be a crib – and a baby was lying inside it. As the man gently lifted the baby he said, "I hope you enjoy doing this."

I didn't. When I drove away from that house that night, I didn't like myself very much.   Even as I tried to rationalize that I was just doing my job, I wanted to quit. A few months later I did.

As I look back on it now, I'm grateful for the

lessons I learned during my brief employment. In addition to the obvious warning to be careful with my own credit purchases, I learned that my personality wasn't a good fit for the furniture financing world. I needed to look in a direction better suited to what made me excited to get out of bed in the morning and go to work.

My advice on jobs is simple. Think deeply about what you want to do in your working life. Don't put this off until you are miserable and feel trapped in a job you can't afford to leave because of a steady paycheck and benefits. Try to match your interests and talents to a job field where you can make a decent living. Learn new skills or seek internships that offer little if no pay. Doors will be opened to you.

Don't expect immediate riches. If you give full effort, you will be amazed by what happens.

Now and Then, Take a Risk

In more than one of those old Westerns, the movie cowboy and his horse end up in a small pond filled with a mysterious liquefied sand. The more the horse and cowboy struggle to get out, the farther they sink. Quicksand! If help didn't arrive soon enough, the horse would be sucked under first, followed by the cowboy. All that would remain was a cowboy hat resting on the surface of the deadly mixture. Then it too would be swallowed.

That kind of scene scared the bejabbers out of me as a kid. As I discovered later in life, it was pure Hollywood invention. Quicksand is actually harmless. The irrational fear of the unknown has always been far more frightening that anything real.

I think of quicksand when I look back on one of the biggest decisions of my life. With the unexpected success of my book *The Richest Man in Town*, I was getting a lot of requests to do paid speaking appearances. It was always my dream to be a professional speaker so it was an exciting time, but I soon discovered the difficulty in balancing the speaking requests with my real job. It quickly became apparent that something was going to have to give.

My job as a university alumni director paid me handsomely. I received a nice benefit package for my pension and insurance. I enjoyed the work and envisioned myself in the job until retirement age. Besides, college campuses are filled with energy and excitement, and the thought of quitting left me with an empty feeling.

Add to this, I had kids in college, a home mortgage with a hefty balance and a ways away before getting my first Social Security check. Giving up a safe and secure job to follow a dream made me worry about the unknown. What if I can't make enough money to have a decent standard of living? What if the economy takes a major downturn? What if no one hires me after a few years? What if I get sick? Keeping me awake at night was a quicksand of my own making.

I needed to change my thinking and start trusting myself. Instead of placing emphasis on failure, I focused on the positive possibilities which included trying to make a difference in the lives of other people, travel and being my own boss. Most of all, I wanted to wake up every morning thrilled to go to work instead of having to go to work.

So, I leaped. And, I have never looked back – not once.

As I reflect on it now, I realize that it would have been easy to play it safe and take no risks. But, I was mortified by the thought of being a cranky old man fueled by bitterness and regret that I never took a chance at doing what I really wanted to do.

When asked in surveys about what they would do differently if they could live their lives over again, many senior citizens say they wished they had taken more risks. Having the benefit of hindsight, they would have stepped out of their comfort zones to do something they wanted to do but were afraid to even try. Taking risks would have brought excitement, adventure and perhaps a whole different outcome in their lives.

No one gets a do-over. But, we can learn from those who came before us – live your dream.

Learn to Accept Appropriate Criticism

When my youngest daughter, Mary Cecile, was three years old I tried to teach her a valuable lesson. It was so valuable that I can't remember what it was.

Anyway, she did something that made me mad so I sat her down at the kitchen table and for the next five minutes I tried to point out the error of her ways. She sat with arms folded and stared straight down at the table in front of her. There was no way she was going to make eye contact with me. After stating her sins against humanity, I resorted to typical parent-speak. "Young lady, do you have anything to say for yourself?"

Mary Cecile looked up from the table and said, "Yeah, I don't like you and I've never liked you."

After a moment of silence, trying to maintain my stature of authority, I busted out laughing. The kid *never* liked me!

It doesn't matter your age, gender or background. No one likes to hear criticism, regardless of how positively it might be spun. For most people, criticism burrows deeply into one's core and lingers, smolders and is never completely forgotten. We remember negative comments and who said them.

When I was eleven years old, my baseball coach ordered all twelve members of our Little League team to stand in line. Early on we nicknamed our coach Hot Dog because he was cocky. Even kids can figure that out.

Our team name was Giants. There were three other teams present – Dodgers, Twins, Yankees – but we were the focus of Hot Dog's wrath that day. In front of forty other kids, Hot Dog walked up and down the line and told every one of us how worthless we were. Then, he grabbed a baseball bat, stopped in front of me and each one of my teammates, pointed the barrel end of the bat toward a kid and said, "You are lazier than hell."

After cutting our four-foot frames down to size, he proclaimed, "They aren't the Giants. They're the Lazier than Hells!" I still remember how crushed and embarrassed I felt at that moment.

A few days after that incident, I learned that a father of one of my teammates had approached Hot Dog and complained about the playing time his kid was getting. That made Hot Dog mad, but instead of yelling at the dad he knew it was easier to take it out on us.

Nice guy, that Hot Dog.

Criticism is a conundrum. Oddly, we don't want it but we need it – well, some of it. Appropriate and measured criticism helps us learn, keeps us from repeating mistakes, introduces us to different perspectives and, in general, can make us better.

But, it's hard to admit a weakness. When someone points out one of our shortcomings, our ego has a tendency to get in the way. I've discovered there is a direct relationship between the size of an ego and the amount of mind closure. The fatter the ego, the less room there is for well-intentioned suggestions and critiques to take root. The "I'm Always Right Syndrome" is a terrible affliction and it affects millions of people (not just talk radio personalities). Personal and business relationships hang in the balance because some people would rather die than admit they might be wrong or need improvement.

Here's a piece of advice for those pig-headed individuals – get over yourselves. You are the only ones who think you do everything right, have all the answers and never make a mistake.

As for the rest of us, weigh the advice offered by others. After moments of honest soul searching you might find merit in what has been shared with you. The first step is accepting the criticism, but the hardest part is taking action to change the behavior. It's a given that change won't be easy as there will be a tendency to slip back into old ways.

Many years ago I worked with a guy named Jaime. He was young, brash and quite full of himself. Jaime was smart but had been poorly trained, especially when it came to providing good customer service. By his own admission, he had been taught to say "no" a lot and rarely went out of his way to do extra things for people. As far as he was concerned, people needed him more than he needed them.

After working side-by-side with Jaime for five years, watching his shenanigans firsthand, I became his supervisor. That's when the fun began. In the beginning we butted heads – often – but it was a fight I wasn't going to lose. In time, he began to accept my suggestions and came to understand how much he was hurting his reputation, thus his career, if he didn't change his ways.

One day Jaime came into my office, looking a little frustrated, and said he wanted to talk. He said he was under a lot of pressure and was starting to revert back to old behavior. Instead of having a helpful attitude he found himself lashing out at people and ignoring requests.

"Jaime, you've arrived!" I shouted. My statement caught him off-guard and he asked me to explain. I said, "For years you had no clue that your behavior wasn't acceptable. Now you see things differently. The reason you are frustrated is because you realize you are falling short of what you expect out of you. I don't need to tell you. So, Jaime, you have officially arrived."

It's fun to watch someone grow.

When You're the Supervisor, Don't be a Jerk

I'm not sure why some seemingly good people morph into egotistical butt-eating aliens when they become managers or supervisors. Maybe it's a power thing and they don't quite know how to handle it. Or, maybe they get turned on by a skewed sense of superiority. Whatever it is, various studies show that the number one reason why people quit their jobs is because of rotten bosses.

The sins of bad bosses include one or more of the following: (1) intimidation; (2) lack of respect shown toward subordinates; (3) harassment; (4) incompetence; (5) the willingness to toss an employee "under the bus" whenever a scapegoat is needed; and, (6) taking full credit for an underling's ideas and hard work. That last one pushes me over the edge.

Do you want to be a leader? Then latch onto four goals:

Get people to see what you see. Call it that "vision thing" if you want, but everyone needs to be on the same page. Subordinates need to know the goals, the rules, boundaries, and consequences, both good and bad. That vision has to be constantly communicated to avoid confusion. Plus, employees need to buy into what you are selling. Try to delegate important work to them so they own the vision, too.

Set a good example. Work as hard, if not harder, than any member of your group. No task should be beneath you. I love it when I see a grocery store manager out in a parking lot picking up trash or corralling shopping carts. Obey all the workplace rules. Never give the appearance of, "Do what I say, not as I do."

Have the ability and guts to make decisions. Groups founder when a boss seems to be hiding underneath a desk. It's critical for organizations, businesses and governments to have direction – and that comes from tough decisions. Be honest with people in assessing their job performance. And, encourage them to be honest with you.

Always be respectful of others. Refrain from talking down to someone, especially in front of other people. Spoken words have the power to uplift or hurt. Positive comments will motivate a group. It never hurts to acknowledge people when they've done good things.

There are thousands of books written on leadership. You can memorize the contents of your favorites, but if you don't treat people with common decency you will never maximize their potential. Nor will you ever be genuinely respected, regardless of your title.

Maybe you don't care what people think. In that case, you should never be a boss.

Beware of Burning Bridges

Oh, the dilemma of spilling your guts.

The momentary euphoria brought on by getting something off your chest – perhaps gaining a little vengeance – has to be weighed against long-term consequences. Besides, you probably don't make your best judgments when you are gripped by anger, jealousy or resentment.

I read an article in which the young author made the contention that it is outdated thinking to worry about burning bridges when it comes to leaving a job. *Really?* Since when did worrying about one's reputation, ending relationships and impacting current or future employment go out of fashion?

Interestingly, most of the people responding to the article agreed with the writer. Why? Because many of them had burned a bridge at some point in their lives and they were seeking justification for what they had done. Guilt, remorse or unintended consequences had caused them to second-guess their decisions to speak up. Yet, the words found in the article gave validation to their actions, thus, some measure of comfort.

Early in my working life and about to quit a job, I decided to burn a bridge. Frankly, it was all new to me and I gave no thought to long term impact. Filled with youthful self-righteousness and a good dose of cockiness, I set about bad-mouthing my boss to his superiors. I didn't care because I was leaving town and I had a whole new world to conquer. Besides, who needed him?

As I painfully discovered – I did.

When I sought new employment, reference calls were made to my previous employer. It's pretty hard to expect glowing comments from a guy whose tail you just scorched. Years later, the embers still smoldered as I was shunned by some of our former colleagues. Personal history, both good and bad, has a tendency to follow you around.

I've never repeated my mistake.

I don't advocate that people have a blanket policy to clam-up when faced with all potential bridge burning moments. On the contrary, situations regarding serious ethical issues, conduct detrimental to the well-being of an organization or illegal activities move things into a different realm completely. There are times when the stakes are so high that you can't stick your head in the sand – at least you shouldn't.

But, personality conflicts, differing views on management styles, perceived slights or hurt feelings – although upsetting – probably don't cut it. You run the risk of sounding petty, selfish, jealous, ignorant or even like a sore loser. Indeed, those are some pretty harsh terms but long after the flames have died out, those things are usually left standing among the ashes.

Here is what I have learned about burning bridges: If you light the match by saying what's on your mind, thus severing ties, you will most likely pay a price. Large or small, now or later, an unknown paymaster dictates the terms. So the real question becomes – what will it cost you?

In the end, you stand a good chance of being the biggest loser. Instead, calm down. Count to ten, a hundred or a thousand. Don't talk. Think.

Something Extra:
Admit When You're Wrong

Okay, a little history lesson here.

During a press conference on November 18, 1973, President Richard Nixon barked, "I'm not a crook!" That was in response to the walls caving in during the height of the Watergate scandal that ultimately brought down his presidency. Nearly twenty-five years later, Bill Clinton looked into the camera on January 26, 1998 and indignantly stated in his well-practiced and now famous line, "I'm going to say this again: I did not have sexual relations with that woman, Ms. Lewinsky."

Both, in the end, were forced to admit failure and apologize to the American people. Neither would have done so had not the preponderance of evidence been so damning. They had no choice.

Witness the number of people you see featured in the media who get caught up in scandals. With few exceptions, they will lash out at their accusers with cries of jealousy, bias or narrow mindedness. They don't have a problem – the accuser, organization or society has the problem. Many attempt to use clever, well-chosen words to show that they are not only right but smart, too. In their thinking, the best defense is a good offense.

In the end, they usually look stupid because they think we are stupid. *BREAKING NEWS* – we aren't stupid.

Pride is a sinister monster that can quickly steal a lifetime of achievement or ruin relationships. Mistakes are a part of life. The key is to limit the number of mistakes we make. But when we make one, the best advice is to take full responsibility, demonstrate genuine remorse and offer a sincere apology. Keep it that simple. Don't muddy the waters during the act of contrition by trying to justify behavior as it sends a message that you aren't really wrong.

In other words, don't talk too much.

*Choose a job you love and you
will never work a day in your life.*

–Confucius

PART THREE:

CHARACTER

Follow the Rules, Even the Stupid Ones

I got caught cheating on a test when I was a senior in high school. Giving into "senioritis" and too lazy to study, I'd written a dozen or so things on a small piece of paper that fit nicely into the palm of my hand. Fifteen minutes into the examination I felt a tap on my shoulder. I looked up and saw the grim face of my teacher, who asked me to follow him outside the classroom.

In the empty hallway, he said, "Give me that piece of paper." I sheepishly handed over my tiny cheat sheet. He studied it for a moment then told me that I failed the exam and there was no reason for me to return to the classroom. He ordered me to go to study hall.

When I look back on it now, I appreciated him not embarrassing me in front of my classmates. It would have been easy for him to make an example out of me in a very public way.

Of course I knew it was wrong to cheat. But, until the moment I got caught, I tried to justify the behavior by telling myself, "Lots of people cheat. It's no big deal."

Well, it *was* a big deal. First and foremost, I was jeopardizing my character. After you cheat once, it becomes easier to cheat again. The ugly reputation of being a cheater is tough to shake. Even now I have a hard time looking into the eyes of my former teacher. I get embarrassed even thinking about it.

Cheating is synonymous with breaking laws or violating company policies. Each day we are presented opportunities to follow established laws and rules or ignore them. It could be something as simple as going ten miles an hour over the speed limit. Or, it could be more complicated things like cheating on taxes or stealing.

I used to have a neighbor by the name of Fred. He was a tall skinny guy around sixty years old and always wore a white T-shirt and blue jeans. Fred took special pride in his yard and seemed to be in love with his lawn mower. I enjoyed visiting with him so every now and then I would interrupt his mowing chores and we would head to the steps leading up to his house. He would sit down, pull a pack of cigarettes out of his pocket, light one up and start down some philosophical path. Fred always seemed to be thinking about life's mysteries.

On one such visit, he sucked in two lungs full of smoke and said something that I have never forgotten.

"The difference between right and wrong is pretty simple," he said. "Most kids can figure it out. It's the application that's difficult."

The wisdom behind those words has stayed with me. So often a clear-cut choice is muddled by peer pressure, financial problems or the "it's no big deal" mentality. Add in a possible short-term gain without thinking about long-term consequences and things can get murky real fast.

When we face the dilemma of breaking the rules, our values – those strongly held beliefs that have been influenced by family, friends, teachers and perhaps religion – rise to the surface. If there is an uneasiness that comes over us, a feeling of discomfort because we are about to step over a forbidden line, chances are the alarms bells are sounding in our value systems and imploring us to pay attention.

Don't ignore the bells. There is a reason why you hear them. Doing the right thing isn't always easy, but in the end, you have to live with you.

Listen to yourself.

Curb the Gossip

A few years after I graduated from college, a defense contractor hired me. All employees had to go through extensive background checks as we were working with classified material. Until we were granted a full security clearance, we just sat in a room and did nothing. The background process usually took six months so that was a lot of sitting around.

One member of the waiting contingent, Carol (not her real name), had gone through almost a year of investigation. We figured she had an ugly skeleton in her closet. During a conversation with her one day, I asked her what her maiden name had been and she told me. The name was well-known to people who lived in my home state – five hundred miles away. So, I asked her, "Are you related to *so-and-so*?" That person was involved in a high-profile crime. Carol said, "Yes, he is my third cousin."

Oh, boy, I had some hot information. When Carol left the room, I gathered everyone together and said, "Evidently the Feds have a computer and when they plugged in Carol's maiden name the bells and whistles went off." Eager for information, the group wanted to know the name. So, I told them and was disappointed that not one person had ever heard of it. Undaunted but wanting to feel self-important – like the best gossipers have a habit of doing – I chose to embellish my findings. I said, "He was the Charles Manson of the North!"

That had their attention. I felt good about myself knowing I'd made such an impression.

Two days later, Carol asked me if I told anyone about who she was related to. Feeling cornered, I knew the jig was up, so I asked her why she wanted to know. She said, "I just had lunch with two of the girls and they wanted to know why I didn't tell them that I was a first cousin to Charles Manson."

What kind of relationship do you think I had with Carol from that point on? It was terrible and I had one person to blame – me.

Why do people gossip? Mental health professionals tell us the answers include envy, resentment, insecurity or the fervent desire to be the center of attention. You might want to toss in a touch of meanness, too. None of those is an admirable trait.

Many of us have been on the receiving end of a gossiper's hurtful tales. When we become aware of what has been said, we are left to wonder who else heard the same thing and the toll it might take on our standing within a group or community. And, the juiciest of the rumors seem to spread like an uncontrolled wildfire – impossible to stop. The key is not to start the fire in the first place or help fan the flames.

Here's my advice on gossip. If you want to pass along questionable stuff but you feel a need to look over your shoulder to see who might be listening ... well, that ought to tell you that your conscience is trying to get your attention. Don't go there.

Of course, there will always be people who don't have a moral compass and will feel free to share whatever they think they know. Rest assured, if you have an acquaintance who gladly shares gossip with you, they will also share gossip about you.

Keep Your Word

If you say you are going to do something – then do it. There are long lasting consequences for promise breakers, and rightfully so.

A few years ago I heard a man speak on this

subject. He said he wanted to be everyone's friend and when he was asked to help with a project he would always give an enthusiastic reply of, "Yessiree, Bob!" Requests to have him work at church suppers or lend a hand to move someone from their home or volunteer to coach a youth baseball team, were all met with a cheerful, "Yessiree, Bob!" The guy said, "I 'Yessiree Bobbed' everybody!"

In reality, he helped with none of it.   Very soon, people stopped asking. In time, nobody wanted anything to do with him so he was shunned. The guy was a victim of his own making.

Fortunately, the man recognized that he was killing what little reputation he had left – just the exact opposite of what he wanted in life. After some real soul searching he made drastic changes and it wasn't easy. A lifetime of big talking and little doing is hard to correct. It's easy to slip into old habits. But, he did change, and his world changed, too.

What does your word mean to you?   Don't believe for a moment that people will forget what you promised them.   Think about the individuals who have made commitments to you and have fallen short.   You remember their names and their promises don't you? I do and I also remember some of the things I failed to do.

My mother taught me a valuable lesson about keeping my word on a bone-chilling January night. I was a substitute paperboy, filling in for a kid who was sick. It was hard to remember the thirty or so houses requiring newspapers as I did the paper beat only one or two times a month. Add to that, the temperature that evening was below zero and a strong north wind made me walk backward whenever I headed in that direction.

Standing in front of the last house on my route, I reached into my pouch and discovered I had two newspapers left. Who did I miss? At that moment I didn't care as my whole body was numb and all I wanted to do was go home get warm. So I did.

Shortly after we were done eating, the phone rang. The guy who didn't get the newspaper was calling and was upset. My mother apologized for the oversight and assured the man that his newspaper would be there shortly. After hanging up, she told me I needed to take the paper across town and make that final delivery. Getting a ride in a car wasn't an option as we only had one vehicle in the family and my father was out of town driving it.

I refused to go. Instead of arguing with me – my mother never argued with anybody – she put on her coat, grabbed the newspaper and walked out into the frozen night. Forty-five minutes later she came back home. Her demeanor toward me, rightly, was as cold as the temperature outside and she didn't speak to me for the rest of the evening.

Just before I left for school the next morning, she said to me a calm voice, "Don't make other people keep your promises."

Her few well-chosen words cut me deeply. It would have been easier had she yelled at me and told me that I was a selfish kid. Yet, watching her walk out into the bitter cold on the previous night and doing what I was supposed to do was an image I couldn't shake. And, many years later, I still can't shake it.

Thanks for the lesson, Mom.

Liars Never Make Good Friends

The biggest problem with habitual liars is that you don't know who you are dealing with. These people have split personalities – and the personalities don't seem to know each other even though they are housed in the same skull. Healthy relationships aren't possible because they are moving targets. In time, liar fatigue sets in, they get heavy and you discard them.

Did you ever notice that you can't win an argument with a liar? They just make up stuff as they go along. And, if they ever find themselves telling the truth, they tell a lie just to get out of it.

By definition, a lie is a statement made to deceive. Have you ever told one of those? How many, huh? And some people are funny in that they "color code" a lie. They will say, "I told a little white lie," as if to purify the lie, thus feeling better about it.

If you stray from the path of truth it will lead to a difficult life. In time, people will learn not to trust you even when you are being honest and factual. There will always be caution about everything you say. That's no way to live.

The noted German philosopher, Friedrich Nietzsche, put it best when he said, "I'm not upset that you lied to me; I'm upset that from now on I can't believe you." Go back and read that statement again. It says everything you need to know on the impact of lying. It can be a lifelong death sentence.

Those who have perfected the art of lying will read what I have written and not see their reflections. And, that's the sad reality of all of this – they even lie to themselves.

Don't be friends with them. Don't hire them. And, for God's sake, don't marry them.

If You Lose Your Reputation, You Never Fully Get it Back

The past isn't always easy to erase.

A person I know, Bill – not his real name – played sparingly on his high school football team. The last game of the season was against a hated rival school, so bragging rights were on the line. An arctic wind made the playing conditions miserable.

Down by three points and only seconds remaining on the clock, Bill's team was driving the football for a game-winning touchdown. The coach called out Bill's name to go into the game. Given the magnitude of situation, Bill was reluctant to go in and tried to act as if he didn't hear the coach. The coach ran over to Bill and screamed, "Get your butt in there!"

Bill grudgingly took the field and a play was called. To his utter horror, it was a pass play and he was to be the intended receiver. The teams lined up and the ball was snapped. Bill ran the pass route perfectly and to his surprise was all alone in the end zone. The quarterback saw the wide-open Bill and heaved the ball in his direction. Everything went into slow motion as the ball floated through the air. All eyes in that stadium were fixed on the ball and the waiting receiver.

As if in a bad dream, the ball hit Bill on the shoulder pad and bounced into the air. He stretched out his hands, but the ball slipped through, hit the ground and tumbled harmlessly away on the frozen field. The game was lost.

Fast forward. Bill completed three tours of duty during the Vietnam War. He retired from the military with many honors after serving his country faithfully for thirty years. And he was delighted when he received an invitation to his fortieth high school class reunion.

After arriving in his hometown, he decided he needed a haircut and headed to the local barbershop to get a trim and catch up on the latest town happenings. Upon walking into the shop he was greeted by the barber and two older local guys. One man said to the other, "Do you know who that is?" The second man said, "No, I don't think so." The first man said, "That's the kid that dropped the pass against *so-and-so* in 1953 and we lost the game."

Most people would agree that something as trivial as a dropped pass by a fifteen-year-old kid in a long-ago football game would be unimportant. I share the story to illustrate the point that many people have long memories. And they get longer as the issue in question gets more important.

Memories are particularly long when it comes to matters of character. If we fail today – morally, legally or ethically – there is a good possibility it will follow us to our graves. Sound harsh? Well, I didn't write the rules.

No matter the professional and personal successes we attain during our lifetimes, if we take a major tumble, we will always have an asterisk by our names. Want proof? Try this list: Tiger Woods, Barry Bonds, Lance Armstrong, Martha Stewart, Rev. Jimmy Swaggart and Pete Rose.

Just the mention of those individuals will cause many people to pause and attach scandal to their names. Each one was highly successful and each one suffered a lapse in judgment, and it cost them dearly. If they can't fully shake the asterisk, do we think we can? I'll guarantee that each one of them would do things differently if given a second chance.

Granted, we shouldn't judge people based on

their worst moments. Added to that, we are urged by pastors, priests and psychiatrists to forgive and forget – for our own mental well-being. Finally, we are a society that promotes the idea of giving people second chances.

The unvarnished truth is that forgiving is the easy part. It's pretty hard to forget.

Don't Look Down on People

I'm guilty of this. There are times when I've made a hasty judgment of a person based on superficial and unimportant things.

It's a common sin and I am a sinner. While making no attempts to try and justify this behavior, I do want to dissect this human shortcoming.

For me, it comes down to intent. When casting judgment, does a person intend to belittle someone – to make them, in their mind, a lesser human being? Does a person seize the moment to make fun of another just for laughs? Is it his intent to place himself on a lofty perch and feel a self-imposed sense of superiority because he thinks he is a little smarter, a little richer, a little better looking or a little more sophisticated?

If so, he's got a problem.

I recall a time when I was working at a university and we were having a lively discussion about a proposed art logo in order to "brand" a certain group. I thought the artwork looked kind of goofy and I said so. No, I didn't use the word *goofy* as I'm a little more socially adept than that. The woman who was championing the idea was offended by my comments and she said, "You are such a *philistine*."

That made me mad.

First of all, I didn't know what *a philistine* was. So I looked up the definition of the word in the dictionary: "Disdainful of intellectual or artistic values." In other words, she was calling me dumb. So I got mad all over again.

To be candid, the real reason I got upset was what the woman did after making the remark. She coughed up a disdainful chortle. Her manner was filled with an air of blue-blooded snootiness. I detest that attitude and it makes me so mad that I start stuttering.

No one likes to feel inferior.

I love Brandt Snedeker, a professional golfer who hails from Nashville. He's a wholesome-looking young man with a big smile. If he was a salesman, I'd buy everything he was trying to sell me.

During a television interview, Snedeker shared a story that I play over and over in my head. He said his family owns a pawn shop in Nashville. Oftentimes, pawn shops are a last refuge for people who need to sell things in order to survive.

When he was a young kid, Brandt and his brother were at the pawn shop watching people come and go. One particular individual caught their attention and after that customer left, Brandt and his brother started to make fun of him. Their father overheard the laughing and carrying on and took the boys aside and said, "You are just one bad decision from being on the other side of this counter."

What a lesson! Each one of us is just one bad choice away from having our lives completely turned upside down. If that happens, what would we want people to say about us – perhaps the same things we said about them?

One more thing and it has to do with the ugly expression "trailer trash." I bristle each time I hear it because I have family members and friends who live in mobile homes – so it becomes personal for me. When someone resorts to using that disparaging phrase, I believe it says a lot more about him than it does about his intended target.

Take a Stand for Loyalty

Loyalty is one of the most important qualities in a friendship. It is the difference maker in distinguishing a friend from just an acquaintance. Never confuse the two.

A friend will have the courage to defend you when the popular thing would be to remain silent. And, a true friend will stand up for you even when you aren't around to hear them do so.

We've all been in the situation before – more often than we want. You are with a group of people and someone says something malicious or unfair about a friend who isn't present. A battle erupts in your soul as you are facing an unwanted dilemma. Do you hold your tongue? Do you say something which could be interpreted as agreeing with the offending statement? Or, do you challenge the person who made the allegation?

The first two options are easy as no feathers are ruffled. A "going along with the crowd" mentality prevents arguments. You don't want to be perceived as a troublemaker or you might lose your place in the group. To speak up might find you on the outside looking in. Thus, silence is safe. Yet, it might not be comfortable.

It's in moments like this that you need to ask yourself a simple question: What kind of a friend am I?

As I reflect on those situations in my own life, I think about some individuals I've met who have a habit of spewing unkind remarks about people as a part of their normal conversations. I've always felt uncomfortable in those moments and wondered if they were going to take a chunk out of me just as soon as I left the room.

Sadly, many people will see this malady in other individuals but will fail to see it in themselves. I've been guilty of this but thankfully there are moments that yank me back on the right track.

A few years ago I was on a phone call with a person who is relatively well-known in the world of public speaking. Out of the blue he said, "V.J., people are stupid." That was quite a statement coming from someone who was making a nice living by preaching the gospel of encouragement. He then proceeded to make a cutting remark about a young woman who hired me for a couple of speaking appearances. Just a few days before, I spoke to that same lady and she had nothing but glowing things to say about him.

I replied, "Well, she sure has nice things to say about you." That caught him off-guard and he didn't know how to respond. He stuttered and gave a slight laugh. For selfish reasons, I hoped I made *him* feel stupid.

In that defining moment I lost a great deal of respect for the man. And, I became very careful about what I shared with him from that point on. I no longer trusted him and decided he could not be my friend as I would always worry about what he would say about me. As the saying goes, the best predictor of future behavior is past behavior.

Choose your friends wisely.

Step Up and Answer for Yourself

When I was five years old, my dad brought home a box of wooden matches. None of us kids had ever seen anything like them before. My brother Terry and I were alone in the kitchen when he grabbed one of those matches and struck it against the wall. We were amazed when it burst into flames. For whatever reason, Terry pulled a tissue from a Kleenex box and lit it on fire, too. It started to burn his hand so he dropped it on the floor and stomped it out with his shoe.

That whole incident intrigued my five-year-old mind. The next morning I woke up early, went downstairs and fetched one of those wooden matches and a Kleenex. I went back upstairs and waited for my brothers to leave the bedroom. When they did, I struck the match and lit the Kleenex. Immediately I could feel the flames singe my fingers so I flipped the Kleenex into the air where it pirouetted one time and dropped in front of me, engulfed in fire. I kicked at it with my bare foot. That was a bad idea – it flew like a blazing hockey puck right underneath a bed.

I dropped to my knees and looked under the bed. Fire was leaping from the tissue onto the cloth of the mattress, and flames began mushrooming in my direction. Scared, I jumped to my feet and ran over and shut the bedroom door. I didn't want anyone to know what was going on. I grabbed a towel and tried to knock down the flames that were burning through the center of the bed, but soon there were too many hot spots spreading everywhere.

I turned around and saw my two-year-old

brother, Stevie, sound asleep on another bed. How he could have slept through all that commotion and smoke I'll never know. I went over and shook him. He sat up at the edge of the bed and his eyes bulged when he saw fire everywhere – the bed, the couch, the curtains ... even our toys were melting. Stevie jumped off the bed and ran to door. He yanked it open and yelled gibberish all the way down the steps. By the way, he's still talking gibberish as he became an attorney.

Within moments my mother came into the bedroom and grabbed me, and we ran downstairs together. A phone call brought out our town's volunteer fire department. Soon we were standing on our lawn watching smoke boiling out of my bedroom windows. Not long afterward, my dad walked up to me – he was highly agitated as he realized the fire was destroying our home and everything in it – and asked, "How did this happen?"

I did the only thing I could think of – I lied.

"I went to the bathroom and shut the door real hard," I said. "I heard something fall in my bedroom and when I went to see what it was and there was a lamp lying on the floor and there were sparks and flames shooting everywhere!"

It must have sounded convincing because it was

reported that way in our town's newspaper. "The cause of the Smith fire was determined to be an electrical problem," read the story.

That lie stuck for twenty-seven years. I finally decided to come clean at a gathering on the evening before my sister's wedding. After asking family members for silence, I said, "Do you remember the fire?" As their heads were nodding, I continued, "Well, I started it."

My mother was sitting directly across from me. She smiled and said, "I'll bet you feel better now." I did, although I regretted that my father didn't live to hear my confession. I can only hope that he would have smiled, too.

When I told my own children about it a few years later, my oldest daughter, Molly, said, "Wasn't grandma really mad at you? You lost practically everything in that fire." My middle daughter, Kelly, came to my rescue by saying, "Grandma shouldn't have been mad at Dad. Grandma should have spanked Terry because he taught Dad how to light that match."

I love that kid.

A reasonable person might exonerate me from blame considering my age at the time. Children often mimic what they see and I certainly did that after following the lead of my brother. Never did I consider an out-of-control fire as a consequence of lighting a seemingly harmless match. Frankly, I didn't know what I was doing.

Yet, I knew what I did was wrong and I lied to cover it up. I wanted to take responsibility for my actions – or at the very least, acknowledge my part in a major incident that affected the entire family. I could have blamed my father for bringing home a box of wooden matches in the first place. Or, I could have blamed my brother for teaching me bad stuff.

Regardless of the circumstances, the simple truth is that my hand lit the match. Mine – no one else's.

Over the twenty-seven years that followed the fire I had witnessed many people fail to accept responsibility for anything. They shared a habit of constantly making up excuses or shifting blame to someone else. Nothing was ever their fault. It's tiring to watch someone who is always playing the victim.

I had watched other people, too, particularly those who accepted responsibility for things that went wrong. Even in difficult moments, one of those people would say, "I'm sorry about this. I will take care of it immediately." In my eyes, they grew in stature.

Taking responsibility is a big part of growing up. And you are never too old to grow. Five-year-olds might be excused for not knowing about responsibility. After all, it took the brain of a thirty-two-year-old to understand that.

Something Extra:
Pick the Right Hero

Neil Armstrong was my hero. Check that – he *is* my hero.

I sat mesmerized in front of our family television set on July 20, 1969, when Armstrong became the first human being to stand on the lunar surface. I went outside my house later that night and stared in awe at the glowing moon, knowing Armstrong and fellow astronaut, Buzz Aldrin were safely tucked away in their lunar spacecraft having completed their historic extraterrestrial hike.

It was an amazing moment and I still get giddy thinking about it. My father's generation had Charles Lindbergh to celebrate after his solo nonstop flight across the Atlantic Ocean in May 1927. Both feats required courage and grit.

Neil Armstrong died on August 25, 2012. You

need to know that I held him in higher esteem at the end of his life than I did on that summer night forty-three years before.

Why? For starters, he shunned the limelight. He felt that too much attention was being given to him and that he was only a part of larger team. He was given the baton by an earlier space flight and it was his job to pass it along. He just happened to have the good fortune of holding the baton on the Apollo 11 mission. That's exactly how he felt.

Armstrong could have made millions of dollars writing books and giving speeches. After all, there would be only one first man on the moon - ever. Armstrong chose not to because he didn't think it was right to profit from a space program paid for by the United States taxpayers. He believed he was given a great gift and it wasn't appropriate to exploit it. Instead of "cashing in" on his celebrity, he became a college professor.

The irony in all of this is that the day before Neil Armstrong died, another Armstrong – Lance Armstrong – was stripped of his record seven Tour de France cycling wins and handed a lifetime ban by the United States Anti-Doping Agency for cheating. His reported worth was estimated to be in excess of one hundred million dollars.

Cheater Armstrong was a first-class bully. He sued and intimidated people who had the courage to step forward to say he was propelled by performance enhancing drugs. Using the power granted to him by his celebrity status, he ran over people. Unwitting corporations flocked to him and stuffed his drug-laden pockets with cash – lots of it.

When Neil Armstrong died, newspapers throughout the country ran stories about a quiet and humble man who became a teacher and lived his final days on a small farm outside Cincinnati. In comparison, when Lance Armstrong dies, within the first paragraph of most news articles it will say he was a disgraced cheater.

One Armstrong had the right stuff, the other one didn't.

Pick your heroes carefully. Do not embrace the new celebrity of the month as you will most likely be disappointed. If you select looks and notoriety over character and courage, you are opting for shallowness over things that are far more important.

Dig much deeper. Better yet, look higher and you might just find your hero soaring above the clouds. I did.

Always do the right thing.
It will gratify some people
and astonish the rest.

–Mark Twain

PART FOUR:

ATTITUDE

Our Most Important Word

Care.

It's the single most important word in the English language.   It even trumps the word "love" because it includes the word love.

Each and every day you are judged by how much you *care*. How much do you *care* about your relationships? How much do you *care* about your job? How much do you *care* about your family?

Here's a truism – you can't teach people to *care*. Conversely, you can teach people *not* to care. It's an interesting thought, isn't it?

Care is the separator of life. It's the difference between being a true friend or just an acquaintance. It's the difference between being an exceptional employee or someone who just shows up for work. It's the difference on having a good marriage or one that might be miserable and on the brink of divorce.

Why?   If you *care* about something you will take extra steps necessary to demonstrate that it is important to you. Your actions will speak because words aren't required. You will do what needs to be done without being told.

Not long ago I was on a flight between San Diego and Minneapolis. Somewhere over the Rocky Mountains, a passenger came forward and discreetly said something to a flight attendant. The flight attendant, showing a look of concern on her face, immediately went to where the man had been sitting. There, she saw a middle-age male passenger slumped over in an adjacent seat. She tried to get the man to respond but it was obvious something was terribly wrong.

The flight attendant quickly moved to a phone and said over the public address system, "Ladies and gentleman, is there a doctor or nurse on board? We have a medical emergency."

Within seconds, a gray-haired man in his mid-fifties stepped forward and said he was a doctor. He was led to the stricken passenger. The doctor quickly assessed the situation and threw the unconscious man's arms around his shoulders, bear-hugged him, and then slowly backed his way up the aisle, dragging the man to the open entry way of the plane. There he carefully laid the man down on the floor.

A second flight attendant produced a large bag of medical supplies. After ripping open the man's shirt, the doctor grabbed something from inside the bag and the next thing I heard was the doctor shouting, "Clear!" He then zapped the man's chest with defibrillator paddles. Placing his ear close to the man's chest to listen for a heartbeat, the doctor realized it didn't work. He grabbed the paddles and again shouted, "Clear!"

Every passenger sat silent and riveted by what we were witnessing. Once again, the doctor bent down and listened to the man's chest. After a few anxious moments, the doctor looked up and said something to the flight attendant. She smiled back at him. It was obvious the man's heart was beating again. An oxygen mask was then placed over the man's nose and mouth.

As the plane continued to Minneapolis, that doctor laid on the floor beside the unknown passenger. Every so often the doctor would whisper something in the man's ear then gently lifted up the oxygen mask to hear his quiet reply.

I marveled at what I was seeing. That doctor could have chosen to remain anonymous and stayed in his seat when the flight attendant called out for help. No one would have known – except him. He chose to take action because he *cared*. All the while the doctor hovered over that man I couldn't help but think that somewhere below us there was a family oblivious to what was happening to their loved one.

After the plane landed in Minneapolis, all the passengers stayed in their seats while an ambulance crew whisked the man off to a hospital. I waited at the gate for that doctor to come off the aircraft. When he did, I stepped forward and shook his hand. I told him it was one of the greatest things I'd ever seen in my life. The doctor gave a slight smile, shrugged his shoulders and simply walked away.

I love people who care.

A Good Outlook is Priceless

When I moved to Kansas City as a young man, I was ready to stake my fortune. I responded to a classified advertisement looking for people to sell solar equipment. It was cutting-edge technology, and we were told that we would be leading the country into a new era of energy independence. Sound familiar?

The truth of the matter is that all we were selling were solar panels encased in a five foot by ten foot metal box that was then bolted down to the roof of a house. Rubber and metal hoses jutted out of all sides of the contraption which resembled a square, squished octopus. I never would have wanted one on my roof.

Every day the sales force would assemble and we would listen to motivational tapes featuring the legendary speaker Zig Ziglar. For an hour we would work ourselves into breast-beating frenzies while hearing 'ol Zig make us believe that the only thing that stood between us and untold riches was our own attitude. Then we were unleashed on the waiting public that, we were told by our management, was just begging to be asked to buy the solar octopus.

Well, we sold nothing. But, the next day we were back listening to Zig again – getting all pumped up again – selling nothing again.

For an hour, though, we were world beaters.

What we were selling was a dumb product and the customers knew it. The best attitude in the world won't make up for stupid. Zig Ziglar wasn't responsible for our failures, or course, but he made them tolerable. At a tough time, he was our greatest source of encouragement.

Cutting through the forest of defeat where excuses ruled the day, the biggest lesson was that a good attitude changes everything. It opens doors and new opportunities. On a personal level, it creates an aura that is contagious and attractive.

I've learned that positive people are a lot more fun to be around than negative people. Want proof? The next time you find yourself in a social setting, remain silent and observe how the ensuing conversation unfolds. A once lively discussion will come to a grinding halt when someone decides to interject something negative or argumentative into the mix, especially if the person persists in his or her demeanor. People will begin to drift away, either physically or mentally. Soon, the offending individual is all alone, left to wonder where everyone went.

The good news is that it is a treatable condition. Over the years I've witnessed many people go through incredible transformations. Having found themselves feeling socially isolated, they've looked into the mirror and saw somebody they didn't like. After serious reflection they changed by (1) thinking less about themselves and more about other people; (2) began asking more questions during conversations and making fewer statements; (3) started thinking before speaking and giving real thought to what to say and how to say it; (4) staying away from negative individuals and the baggage they brought with them; and (5) worked hard on looking at the positive things about situations rather that dwelling on the negative side.

I'm inspired by positive people – and you can find them everywhere.

On a January day several years ago, I was walking down an icy sidewalk when I decided to duck into an art museum to escape the numbing sub-zero temperature. Upon entering the building, my eyeglasses immediately fogged over. People with eyeglasses understand this all-too-frequent occurrence and long for the days of no eyewear.

After removing my glasses, I looked up and saw the welcoming face of an older woman who was sitting at the information desk. She was a volunteer at the museum. I said, "Can you believe how stinking cold it is?" She smiled and replied, "Yes, but isn't the sunshine wonderful?"

Her remark caught me off-guard and I didn't know how to respond.

Two months later, I found myself walking outside that same art museum in a fierce snowstorm. Cold, wet and wearing a coat caked over with half-frozen snow, I again sought refuge in the building. Once more I was greeted by "Miss Sunshine." Brushing off the white powdery stuff that was sticking to my coat and looking for a little sympathy, I said to her, "It's terrible out there!"

The cute lady said, "What a blessing. We need the moisture."

Another few months passed and I had to attend a meeting at the art museum. Spring winds were in high gear clocking at forty miles per hour. It took both hands to open the museum door. After slipping inside, I heard the door slam shut hard behind me.

Slightly disheveled and substituting my hand for a comb, I quickly tried to get my hair back in order. I glanced up and there sat the same woman. I thought – this time I've got her! In my mind, there was nothing good she could say.

"That wind is awful!" I said.

True to her nature, she grinned, winked her eye and said, "It keeps the bugs off, you know."

Take a Moment and Listen to Your Elders

When my oldest daughter Molly was four years old, her daycare class visited a local nursing home. She said it was fun to go there but wondered why old people liked to pat kids on head so much. And, ever the rules follower, Molly told me that she strictly adhered to the stern warning issued on dealing with the senior residents.

"Our teacher told us not to bite them, pinch them or stomp on their feet," beamed Molly.

Not inflicting bodily pain aside, the teacher was simply telling the kids to be nice to the older generation. That's great advice regardless of age. Special deference to the elderly shows our compassion and civility.

Of course there are moments when our respect for the aged is challenged. Getting behind a slow octogenarian driver on a roadway or standing in a store checkout line patiently waiting for a confused gray-haired lady to complete her transaction sometimes tests us. Then we remember that one day we will be old, too, and we hope that a modicum of age tolerance never goes out of style.

That's a concept not always understood when you are young. I'm reminded of a visit to Harvard University one October. The prestigious college was a stopping point for a touring group that consisted of forty older members of my alma mater's alumni association. The tour guide wanted a group picture so he directed us to stand on the steps leading up to a grand old building located at the core of the beautiful campus.

After huddling us together, he stepped back to snap the photo. Before he did, he looked to his left and saw a group of students walking down the sidewalk which passed directly in front of us. The tour guide politely asked the students, "Could you hold up for a moment while I take this picture?"

One young lady broke from the pack, barreled down the walkway without breaking stride and huffed, "I will not be disrespected!"

Disrespected? The impetuous young woman appeared to be confused by the word's very definition. Her reaction should have been, "Hey, it's a bunch of cute old people. Let's give them their special moment."

Let's get down to the basic issue: respect. The debate rages on whether respect should be earned or just given. Respect earned, you have proven your keep. If given, unless you mess up you are worthy of maintaining the distinction. This turns into an endless, tiring and non-winnable argument. Instead of getting bogged down in definition it's best to look at what it truly should be: common decency.

A vital part of that common decency, especially as it applies to the senior generation, is taking the time to listen. The act of listening to someone implies that their lives have relevance – they matter. And, even though their most productive years might be behind them, they still have something to offer.

Besides, we learn a lot by listening as many of our preconceived notions about a person are proved wrong through discovery.

This lesson was front and center when I spoke to a group of teachers in northern Minnesota. A throng of faculty and staff were milling around a half an hour before the start of the program. In the midst of the chaos, I was approached by a man who appeared to be in his mid-sixties. It was obvious he was upset and he said, "Where the hell is the men's bathroom?" I told him I didn't know. He said, "They try to take care of all these damn women so they put a temporary sign over the men's bathroom and have made it into another women's bathroom. I gotta pee and I don't know where to go."

Not knowing what to say to him, I simply shrugged my shoulders. As he turned to walk away, he said, "This is my last year of teaching before I retire and I can't wait to get the hell out of here."

My first thought was that he was a cranky old man. My second thought was that I was glad he wasn't *my* teacher.

Fast forward to the program. Shortly after I began to speak, I noticed the cranky guy sitting in the audience directly in front of me. It was a little awkward and uncomfortable at first. As I proceeded to share my story I witnessed an amazing transformation. The once-prominent scowl had been replaced by a sad, teary-eyed face. I didn't know what to make of it.

Within minutes of completing my talk, the veteran teacher walked up to me with his hand extended. He said, "I'm sorry about being upset when I met you earlier. I didn't know you were the speaker." Then he shared a critical detail. "My wife died a month ago after a long bout with cancer. We were married for forty-years. I just feel lost," he told me.

I made a hasty judgment about the man based on our original encounter and I really didn't know him or his background. But, after listening to him and being made aware of his loss, I came away with an entirely different opinion. My disdain was replaced by empathy.

Take time and listen. By offering a compassionate ear, we help validate someone's existence. In essence, we are saying that other lives matter, they count – and aren't just taking up space. But, it is far from a one-way street. The listener has the opportunity to gain a mentor, maybe extract a little wisdom and spawn a new friendship.

My life took a complete detour when I met Marty, a little old man who ran a cash register at Wal-Mart. Given his advanced age and his job, that wouldn't seem possible. Yet, when I took the time to get to know him my whole world changed. Listening to him share his modest background and his thoughts on life gave me a newfound appreciation on some of the simple joys we often overlook.

I'll say it again: It's amazing what can happen if you pay attention.

Free Muscles Never Get Sore

I was a skinny little kid. Genetics and high competition for a finite amount of food among four brothers and four sisters have a tendency to keep you on the thin side.

Not happy with the look of my twelve-year-old body, I vowed to do something about it. While reading a comic book one day I saw an advertisement featuring Charles Atlas. Just his name gave me the shivers.

Sporting minuscule tight leopard shorts, the muscular and bronze-bodied Atlas stared up from the page and proclaimed, "I can make YOU a new man, too, in only fifteen minutes a day!"

He had the right credentials as the ad said he was holder of the coveted title, "The World's Most Perfectly Developed Man." My excitement hit a fever pitch when it stated, "Just watch your scrawny chest and shoulder muscles begin to swell ... those spindly arms and legs of yours bulge ... and your whole body starts to feel alive, full of zip and go!"

Oh boy, I wanted zip and go!

And, I could have it all FREE! Yes, the ad assured me that for the price of a postage stamp I could have a perfectly sculpted body. Girls would flock to me and my friends would be jealous – all courtesy of just a postage stamp. So, I sent away for the FREE thirty-two-page booklet and waited for my muscles to show up.

A few weeks later the booklet arrived. My joy quickly melted into disbelieving horror as I was introduced to the mysterious concept of Dynamic Tension. In a series of photographs and diagrams I was instructed on self-resistance exercises.

Exercising? Who said anything about

exercising? I was going to have to sweat? You've got to be kidding me! That advertisement didn't say a thing about doing weird contortions with my body, grunting and feeling physical pain. No, it said I could have FREE muscles. There was no way I was going to give up my spare time and push against heavy objects. Girls weren't *that* important.

It was an early life lesson. If I wanted something, a certain price had to be paid. If I wasn't willing to pay the price then I couldn't have what I wanted. Even though I wanted muscles, I made the choice that I wasn't going to put in the effort to get them.

We place great value in something when we work hard to get it. Conversely, if we are merely given something, outside a gift from a loved one or friend, chances are we won't treasure it in the same way.

A great example is when you use your hard-earned money to buy a car. You wash, polish and vacuum it, taking special care to make it look good. It becomes a source of pride. And, there are times when you walk away from the car but pause for a minute to look back at it and feel an enormous sense of satisfaction knowing that it's yours and you earned it.

And, if you look close enough, you will see your reflection in a window. It's a poignant moment and serves as a reminder that your work and sweat made that car a reality.   You did it.

It's All Water

My grandfather died when I was just shy of being five years old. I don't remember much about him other than he wore a huge, flesh-colored plastic hearing aid that seemed to devour one of his ears. A small white wire connected it to a battery pack which could be seen bulging from within his shirt pocket.

It looked official.

But, he didn't seem to be able to hear anything except for small children who ran repeatedly in front of his recliner while he was taking a nap. Abruptly awakened, he would grab his walking cane and trip the next kid who came scurrying along. Then the kid got a tongue lashing on the need to allow old people to get some rest.

The son of a Civil War veteran, my grandfather witnessed from afar our country's forays into the Spanish-American War, World War I, World War II and the Korean War. He watched as noisy automobiles replaced the horse and buggy. Flying machines like airplanes and rockets intrigued him. He didn't live long enough to see a man on the moon, but I doubt it would have surprised him.

What would have shocked him, I'm sure, is the idea of people paying four dollars for a bottle of water.

Now, I appreciate the convenience and portability of a bottle of water. Plus, I know water is a far healthier alternative to a bottle of sugar-or chemical-laden soda. But what I don't get is why some brands cost twice as much for the same amount of water.

One day I stopped a young lady who had just grabbed a $1.89 bottle of cleverly packaged water. I asked her why she picked that brand over the stuff that was half the price. She looked at the bottle then back at me and said, "It must be better 'cause it costs more."

I'm thinking she wasn't the valedictorian of her class.

Some companies use images of snow-capped mountains and pristine rivers to convey a sense of nature's purity. Mega-corporations invented names like Dasani (Coca Cola) and Aquafina (Pepsi Cola) to give a little panache to their marketing schemes.

The truth is that the water for both Dasani and

Aquafina comes out of a tap. Filtered city water isn't very glamorous but the good news is that municipal water systems are highly regulated by the federal government. You can get pretty much the same thing from your kitchen sink.

At a shop in the Tampa airport, I studied a bottle of Icelandic Glacial water that cost a whopping $4.49. Those Icelanders are devious little devils, too. I read the fine print on the label and it was noted that the water did not actually come from a glacier. P.T. Barnum had it right: There's a sucker born every minute. And a lot of them are buying expensive bottled water.

Maybe the funniest thing about bottled water is the expiration date. Leave it to man to put an expiration date on something that has been around since the beginning of the planet.

Do you want to save some money? Then pack your own water. Here's a novel idea – the same one you knew as a kid – take a drink from a water fountain. It's from the same source. And it's free.

There are No Secrets for a Happy Life

I smile whenever I see a book extolling some newly discovered secret about having a cheerful life. The same goes for a motivational speaker who claims to have stumbled onto a mystical vault, and upon opening it a great secret is revealed.

Really?

Let's get this straight – I'm not mocking books with positive messages or speakers who give audiences an emotional lift. I've written such a book and I speak to make a living. For me to malign those things would be more than a little foolish.

My issue isn't the content – it's the premise. It's a goofy idea to think that an unknown concept has been miraculously dredged from the bottom of human consciousness and revealed to a waiting universe.

BREAKING NEWS – there aren't any secrets on having a happy life! And, I don't care what kind of clever marketing stuff is thrown at me, it isn't sticking on my flypaper. It's all right there in front of us if we care to pay attention and do the work.

Sitting around and wishing for happiness

isn't going to cut it. Seeking happiness is a different thing altogether. To seek requires effort on our part. Remember, the Declaration of Independence states that our unalienable rights include life, liberty and the *pursuit of happiness.* In other words, pursuit requires movement and we can't sit lazily on a rock hoping to get hit on the head by a magical happy stick courtesy of the merry fairy. It isn't going to happen.

What are the ingredients for a happy life? For starters, hang around happy people. Stay away from the cranky folks. If a person chooses to get married, he or she needs to find someone who thinks more about positive things than negative things. Be leery of a nagger, no matter how good-looking he or she might be; one day the looks will be gone but the nagging will remain. Avoid fault finders; too, they will always steal your energy.

Find meaningful work as it will give a purpose to life. Reach out and help others who are less fortunate. Don't just suck air – commit to making a difference. Make it a priority to be nice to people, even if they aren't nice to you. Look around and discover all the gifts we have been given – and be sincerely grateful for each one. Embrace the future as there are so many good things to look forward to.

If we have an upbeat attitude, then we are in for a great ride. People who choose the opposite path are guaranteed a very small funeral.

Ground Those Angry Birds

Outside of Thanksgiving, it's never good to give or receive the bird.

Giving someone the finger is meant to be a provocative statement. Rather than unleashing the supernova of all cuss words, a person lets their middle finger do the talking. Sure, it might be mysteriously satisfying or funny at the moment, but the recipient probably won't see it the same way.

I don't know of a single person whose image has been enhanced by shooting the bird. Yet, famous people have been flipping-off folks for years. In 1976, Vice President Nelson Rockefeller smiled and gave a group of young demonstrators the finger at a campaign stop in New York. He said he was simply "responding in kind." Johnny Manziel of the Cleveland Browns, better known as Johnny Football, raised the one-finger salute toward Washington Redskins players and the

NFL fined him $12,000. That pales in comparison to the fine levied on the late Bud Adams, owner of the NFL's Tennessee Titans. His use of both middle fingers cost him a whopping $250,000. Pop stars, rock stars and some Hollywood celebrities use the gesture just to keep their names and faces in the news.

I'm not sure what it says about the state of the human condition that the act of flipping-off someone is so much a part of pop culture and society in general. Have we advanced or regressed?

Regardless of age, everyone knows what it means. When I was a kid, I was standing on our lawn with my cousin Tom. In the distance we could see his dad driving down our street. Tom said his father was kind of dumb and didn't understand things. When his dad pulled up in front of our house, Tom said, "I'll show you what I mean."

Tom walked over to the driver's side of the car, got close to the window and flamboyantly flipped-off his old man. He used two hands – it was a *double flip-off*. His dad smiled back at him. Tom looked at me and said, "See?"

His dad got out of the car and walked over to Tom and promptly swatted him on his butt. "Don't you ever do that again!" he shouted.

Tom's dad was smarter than he thought.

It seems that people in cars are most apt to use the gesture. I suppose it's because they know they can make a quick get-a-way – sort of a "drive by flip-off."

A few years ago I was driving a large motor home down a busy Interstate 35 just north of Des Moines. I noticed a car to my immediate right coming down an onramp and trying to merge into traffic. Checking my rearview mirror, I realized I couldn't move to the next lane because there were two cars in my path. Since the motor home was somewhat of a beast, I wasn't able to hit the brakes because it takes time for 30,000 pounds to slow down – so I stayed the course.

The driver of the car that was trying to merge into traffic was not happy. Within a minute, he pulled up on the left side of my rig and honked his horn several times. He wanted me to look at him. I glanced to my left and couldn't believe what I was seeing. A young man sitting in the back seat was giving me the finger. A young woman in the front passenger seat joined him in wishing me a happy birthday. Then – and this is the kicker – the driver stretched his body across the passenger seat, he had his face almost against the window, and he was shooting me the bird, too. It was a *three finger flip-off*!

I was amazed by the sight of it. I smiled and waved back at them – a traditional wave and acted as if I didn't understand the message they were sending me. They sped away and I'm sure the ensuing X-rated conversation centered on old drivers and that we ought to get the hell off their road.

Eventually we will.

Fly the Friendly Skies

I am not a food prude. I'm thirty pounds overweight and crave spicy chicken wings. If I have to be marooned on a desert island with only one food to live on for the rest of my life, I'll pick Old Dutch plain potato chips.

Yes, I'm that pathetic. The potato chips *are* tasty, though.

My food shortcomings aside, I detest it when someone walks onto a commercial airplane carrying an oil-stained brown or white bag filled with greasy, smelly food. Onion rings are the worst, followed closely by french fries. A cloud of stench will hover in the plane's cabin for the entire duration of a flight.

For me, this whole thing is akin to the argument over smoking. That being, "Your freedom ends where my nose begins." Fellow passengers don't have the luxury of moving to a different seat to flee from the offensive odor. In the closed in quarters of an airplane, everyone owns the same air. So, stay away from the smelly stuff, please.

Civility shouldn't end with food choices. Squeezing two hundred strangers into an airplane often tests patience and understanding. Take the recliner mechanism on the seat. Ten years ago while on a flight from Phoenix to Minneapolis, I moved my seat back and the woman directly behind me shouted, "No you don't! I am doing work back here. Move your seat back – now!" Embarrassed, I quickly returned the seat to its upright position. As we flew on I gave a lot of thought to that brief encounter because, frankly, it made me mad. She could have said, "Sir, I'm doing some work back here. I'd appreciate the extra room." In other words, saying something a little more positive would have been better for both of us because her reaction immediately put me on the defensive. Based on that encounter, I now ask the person directly behind me if it is okay to put back my seat. I don't take it for granted.

Another test on a plane is the incessant chatterer. Through the years I've heard many passengers talk continually from takeoff to landing. Regardless of the flight's duration, they never wear down. It's pretty hard to take a nap if you are in earshot of them – especially the loud ones. I'm convinced that some people talk loud because they feel the need to be heard over the roar of the plane's engines. I suggest a good pair of headphones.

Of all the difficult situations I've encountered on a plane, the number one issue is the impact of crying children. A screaming child presents a challenge for almost everyone – except the pilots who sit behind closed doors. For starters, babies aren't making conscientious decisions to cry – they only know that they feel hot, cold, bored or hungry, have a wet diaper or that their ears hurt. Most passengers understand this and cut a little slack for a parent who is actively trying to quiet a child. The parent acting oblivious to the wailing of their urchin – thus giving the appearance of not caring about how it is affecting fellow flyers – is viewed in a whole different light.

Not long ago I was on a two-hour flight where a small child cried the entire time. The constant bawling completely changed the mood on the plane.

The passengers seemed to go from happy to slightly amused to upset to angry and finally downright exhausted. When we landed, people started clapping – it was that bad.

When I left the plane and walked-up the jet bridge leading to the terminal, I noticed the mother of the child and she was holding the toddler closely and swaying back and forth, kissing the now quiet baby on the forehead over and over again. The mother had her back to us and stared at the wall which was only inches from her face. Embarrassed and hurt, she was crying as she was well-aware of what happened on the plane.

Seeing this and feeling sorry for her, I walked over and put my hand on her shoulder. I said, "Your baby doesn't know what it's doing. It's okay." The mom whispered, "Thank you," but she continued to look straight ahead, crying softly and swaying back and forth.

Patience and understanding are essential human qualities in all facets of life – especially on planes. And, maybe a good set of headphones, too.

Never Buy a Potato Chip
That Supposedly Looks Like Jesus

Every so often the news brings us stories about people claiming to find the image of Jesus burned into a piece of toast. Or the bark of a tree. Or on a potato chip. This sends a few believers into a tizzy as they take it as some type of heavenly sign. Mercenary types put the images up for public auction – business is business, you know.

Yet those images on the potato chip, the toast or pancake don't look like the same guy. Sure, they all have beards, mustaches and long hair – but that doesn't make them Jesus. I've seen lots of guy who looked like that. Most of them were smoking pot and grooving to music. I'm thinking Jesus didn't do that.

The Shroud of Turin made a better case for reverence. For centuries, scientists, historians and theologians have hotly debated the authenticity of that ancient relic, which shows the face and body of a male human being and is touted by many as the burial cloth of Jesus.

Radiocarbon testing done in 1988 dates the

cloth to be manufactured around 1300 AD. A later study disputes that 1988 testing. Of course, science and religion often clash. Heck, religions clash with other religions. John Calvin, a leader in the Protestant Reformation, wrote the shroud mystery was not to be believed because St. John penned there were two cloths used to wrap Jesus, not one. The faithful push all of that aside as they fervently believe the garment is real and shows us the image of Christ.

All of this begs the question: Who actually knows what Jesus looked like? Answer: No one.

To me, Jesus is the most significant person ever to have walked on the face of the Earth. His brief life has shaped beliefs, cultures, laws and the lives of countless people for more than two thousand years. No one has had a greater impact on the human race. Even level-headed atheists and agnostics have to recognize that fact.

The Shroud of Turin aside, I have a hard time understanding why people would want to trivialize Jesus' life by claiming that his image can be found on a Frito chip or slice of Wonder Bread.

I don't buy it. And, you shouldn't buy any of it, either.

Something Extra:
Tune In to the Whistler's Joy

A lot of people think whistling is just an obnoxious noise. For some, the high-pitched sounds and monotonous repetition of the same four to six notes places whistling right behind humming on the list of all-time most irritating musical sounds – just above the kazoo.

But, there are times when we encounter an excellent whistler and, at least for a moment, we marvel at the sound of it.

Whistling fell into disfavor at about the same time that rock and roll music kicked in. Most families in the 1950s did not have some type of musical device to play recordings – only the home radio. So, people made their own music by either singing or whistling as neither one cost any money.

Everything changed with the advent of the LP (long playing) records and availability of hi-fidelity stereo phonograph systems. The sound quality was revolutionary and you didn't have to wait for your favorite singer or song to randomly appear on the radio. You just slapped on a black vinyl disc and sat back and listened to the likes of Elvis Presley and the Big Bopper. If someone tried to whistle along, they were promptly greeted with, "Will you shut up?" That's how it worked in my house and I speculate many others. Thus came the enigmatic ending of the golden age of whistling.

I just made all of that up.

Getting past my speculation on the demise of whistling, let me offer another theory on a related topic – there are no unhappy whistlers. On this I am serious.

I've given this a lot of thought. Whenever I hear someone whistling I notice a bounce in their step and a generally happy attitude.

A year ago, I was walking down the main street in my hometown and I heard someone whistling a hearty tune. I glanced to my left and saw a man I know sweeping the sidewalk in front of his white stucco restaurant. The guy's broom darted, jumped and scooted all in rhythm to his energetic, nonstop, happy whistling. It seemed to be a choreographed dance of love between a man and his broom.

Mixed emotions were running through my head as I knew the man only had a few more months left to live. An aggressive cancer was robbing him of his physical health, yet it couldn't steal his mind. So, there he was, completely wrapped in his self-spun cocoon of blissful joy and he didn't seem to have a care in the world.

In that moment I wondered if I was going to be a happy warrior when I fight my last fight.

My thinking about whistling changed after that encounter. Rather than considering it an annoyance I now smile and celebrate the whistler's joy – regardless of the tune.

Most folks are as happy as they make up their minds to be.

–Abraham Lincoln

PART FIVE:

CONNECTING

Acknowledge an Act of Kindness

Someone holds a door open for you. An observant shopper moves his grocery cart to the side in a shopping aisle so you can squeeze by. A kind soul slows down or stops his car and motions for you to merge your car in line in a crowded parking lot after an athletic event or concert. Someone allows you to cut in line at your local post office, thus saving you time at his expense.

What is your reaction in those situations? Some say or mouth a thank you. Others smile and nod in appreciation. And some will give a simple "thumb's up" sign.

Or maybe there's nothing – no reaction at all.

I believe I speak for millions of people when I vent my frustration on those sour individuals who don't have the common decency to even modestly recognize or acknowledge a moment of kindness.

Not long ago I was in Montana and I saw a young man waiting to exit a gas station. I stopped my car a good distance from the rear end of the truck in front of me as an obvious sign to the guy that I wanted

125

him to cut in front of me. He did, but he didn't even look at me. No acknowledgment, no wave, no nothing.

In Washington D.C., I brought my rental car to a halt and motioned to a smartly dressed man and his female companion to cross the street even though they weren't in a crosswalk. The woman smiled and gave a sheepish wave. In complete contrast, the man looked straight ahead and never stopped talking. I suppose he was bantering about his important work and didn't want to be bothered with such small things. Pompous people like to think it's all about them.

Selfishness has no borders. A fellow in Australia sent me an email and begged me to send him a book. He said he had been wiped out by a nasty divorce and was emotionally and physically drained and zapped of his resources. Further, since he only had $2.56 to his name, he was unable to buy a book but wrote that he needed to find some inspiration. Taken by his sad account, I sent him a book and included a note of encouragement. The international postage cost me twenty dollars.

Did he send a note back to me? Nope. Perhaps his lack of appreciation factored into his divorce.

The people who do good deeds aren't looking for applause or slaps on the back. They do those things because their hearts tell them to do so. But, in time, even the most generous spirit can get a little hardened or jaded when the recipients repeatedly fail to acknowledge moments of cordiality.

Every act of kindness given to you deserves some type of positive response. That's how the universe works. If you don't like it, move to a different universe.

Healing Begins With an Apology

I know people who would rather die than apologize. You do, too.

Some believe it's a sign of weakness to say "I'm sorry." It's hard to get past their egos and humble themselves – believing they will be giving up their position of strength. In their minds, to apologize is an admission of failure and may be a little humiliating.

That pride things starts to raise its ugly head.

I've discovered that it might not be a simple matter of hard-headedness. I think there is another reason for this attitude. I learned it at a school.

Speaking to a group of high school students one day, I posed two related questions. First, I asked how many of them were waiting for an apology from someone. Every student raised a hand. Then, I asked how many of them needed to apologize to someone. After a squeamish moment, a few courageous souls lifted their hands. Seeing this, over half the students did the same.

I asked them why they wouldn't go to that person and apologize. A young girl replied, "I know this might sound dumb, but I don't know how to do that." When I looked to the other students to gauge their reactions to the statement, I noticed many were nodding their heads in agreement.

As I reflected on that moment, I realized that I was well into my thirties before I grasped the technique and the cleansing power of an apology.

It's important to take a complicated situation and try to make it simple. And, there needs to be some urgency about it. The first ingredient is sincere remorse – that usually can't be faked. A quick or flippant "I'm sorry" won't do anything other than sending the offending person deeper into the doghouse.

There needs to be an acknowledgment of the hurtful statement or unkind act and a request for forgiveness. If a person tries to make an excuse for the behavior or tries to justify the behavior, then there is no real remorse. Worse, the person is saying it really wasn't their fault and they will be headed back to the doghouse.

Of course, some people like the doghouse.

Forgiveness Requires Real Work

Most major religions have forgiveness as one of their central themes. Libraries are filled with books written by mental health professionals about the personal health benefits of forgiveness. Even the English poet Alexander Pope weighed in on this three centuries ago when he penned the famous phrase, "To err is human; to forgive, divine."

I'll wager that lots of religious leaders, psychiatrists and benevolent wordsmiths have a few people in their own non-forgiving closets. In reality, it's a lot easier to talk about forgiveness than to actually put it into practice. Even after the obligatory "I forgive you" statement has been uttered, it has to pass the test of time.

I've known many people who felt a great burden lifted because they have forgiven someone. They have moved on. I deeply admire those people as they seem to have found inner peace.

Unfortunately, I know many people who are going to hold a grudge until they die. I feel sorry for them, so wrapped in their anger. Have you ever noticed that those people aren't a lot of fun to be around? They share the same stories over and over again, seeking pity to help reinforce their bitterness. For some, there seems to be an odd joy in remaining stuck as they see it as a way of getting noticed.

It's hard to truly forgive someone, especially if you have been seriously wronged.

Moving forward requires real work. There is no magic pill to make everything better. Yet, you own it – no one can do this for you. Seek counseling with a trusted friend, a professional or member of the clergy. Read material on forgiveness and its benefits. Give serious reflection to how the anger is holding you back – dang it, do something!

Many years ago I worked with a man who had a great motto: forgive and remember. It was an honest assessment on this whole idea of forgiveness. You probably can't forget what was done to you, but coming to terms with it and letting go of resentment will help you remove what is holding you back.

Don't stay stuck.

Misery Can't Stand to be Alone

Some people are so willing to share their troubles. Perfect strangers, within moments of meeting you, will pour out their problems like a broken faucet.

I'm reminded of what a woman shared with me after she had major surgery. As she lay in bed just hours after the procedure, groggy and in pain, she encountered two hospital aides at different times who felt compelled to tell her their own misfortunes. One babbled incessantly about her dastardly former employer. The other droned on and on about the lousy husband she divorced. Neither of the aides gave much thought to anything else other than their own weary lives.

Shortly after leaving the woman's room, one of the aides entered an adjacent hospital room. True to form, she immediately began telling the exact same story to the poor patient lying hostage on the bed.

Former football coach and sports analyst, Lou Holtz, had it about right when he said, "Never tell your problems to anyone. Twenty percent of the people don't care and the other eighty percent are glad *you* have them."

That may seem a bit harsh but Lou has a point. It isn't that people aren't compassionate, but you have to pick your spots in life. There are times to talk about your problems. All the time isn't a viable option. Friends, family members, co-workers and even strangers will gradually drift away from the relentless sea of negativity. It's just too much to handle.

If you encounter such a person, remain silent. Don't say a word. Try to avoid eye contact as it will only encourage him or her. Such a person will eventually wind down and move on.

Want to kill a few hours and make a lifelong friend? Then take the bait. And good luck.

Make Yourself Useful to Your Neighbors

I was shocked to learn that only one in four individuals volunteers his or her time in service to other people. Growing up in a small town, I had the impression that just about everyone volunteered in some capacity or another. I was wrong.

Hearing that statistic got me thinking about

my old high school biology teacher, Mr. Greco. More than forty years ago he broke from his typical messages about human anatomy and staph infections to tell us there were two types of people in this life. First, he said, there are *the breathers.* They stand on the sidelines, just suck in air, don't participate and watch the world unfold in front of them. They usually have an opinion about things and are the first to complain and last to lift a finger to help.

Second, there are *the bleeders*. Rather than standing idly by and watching things happen, they make things happen. They roll up their sleeves, pitch-in and give precious time to try and make a difference in their communities. Along the way they might sweat a little, grow calluses on their fingers or get cut up by work worth doing. Their lives have real purpose.

What drives people to be bleeders and not breathers? Sure, there are those who do it to strengthen a resume, enhance a social network, create a positive image or develop business skills. Honestly, I'm okay with all of that just as long as the work gets done.

I have long admired people who run for public office – especially those at the local level where you get a title but no salary. It takes some real guts to offer your name for consideration. The candidates are essentially saying, "Okay world, here I am – warts and all. What do you think?" Spurred on by a sense to serve, they open themselves to inspection and criticism. It is not an easy thing to do.

I'm a little old school when it comes to motive. I'd like to think that people who step forward are driven by an unselfish concern for the welfare of others. I know that's altruistic thinking for some, but I've discovered there is a profound sense of joy in giving time and treasure and expecting nothing in return – except to live with yourself. It's giving in its purest form.

Just a final thought on volunteering: If you say you are going to help, then follow through on your word. Over the years I've witnessed many well-intentioned people fall short of their promises. They end up looking bad. Don't commit to something unless you are prepared to deliver.

Before You Speak, Know the Facts

Making assumptions seems to be a national pastime. And, jumping to conclusions is about the only exercise some folks get. The net result is that a lot of people end up looking rather foolish. I speak from experience.

When I was in my early twenties I found myself on the tree-lined shore of a pristine lake in the Black Hills of South Dakota wanting to do a little trout fishing. While trying to bait my fishing hook with an uncooperative worm I looked to my right and standing a hundred feet away was an older fisherman, perhaps in his mid-sixties, patiently standing and staring at the rippling blue water.

Using fishermen speak, I yelled, "Are the fish biting?" The man looked at me, said nothing and turned his eyes back to the water. Filled with the impertinence of youth, I wanted him to pay attention so I barked, "*I said* are the fish biting?" The guy turned his head and just stared at me. Smugly I said, "What's the matter, cat got your tongue?"

The man paused for a moment then pulled back

the collar on his shirt and pointed to the tracheotomy hole cut into the base of his neck. He couldn't speak. Neither could I. At that moment I just wanted to run away.

Some hard lessons don't always take hold.

I left a phone message for a man with a request to return my call. A day passed and then another; still no reply. So, I dialed him again and getting no answer I left a message with a little more urgency in my tone. Several more days went by and I didn't hear from him.

My patience exhausted, I called him once more and this time he answered. Thinking I needed to take him to task, I said, "I called you a week ago and you never called me back. *Why are you ignoring me*?" After a moment of silence, the man told me his father died unexpectedly and he just returned from burying him.

I wanted to run away again.

In a digital and fast paced world, everything is being downsized and abridged – including our patience. We have grown accustomed to instant everything. Emailing, once a cutting-edge communication, is now trumped by texting and tweeting because of brevity and speed. And, we demand quick answers. So when the answers don't come fast enough, we sometimes start making stuff up.

Sadly, the truth is usually a victim in the drive for expediency. Question: What do you have when you don't know all the facts? Answer: Nothing. A partial truth isn't the truth.

Slow down and get the facts before you speak. Assume nothing. You can save yourself a lot of trouble and embarrassment if you practice a little patience.

Take a breath.

Beware the Truth Specialists

Often there is a giant divide between perception and reality.

I learned that valuable lesson when I worked in a labor relations office at a large manufacturing facility in Kansas City, Missouri. Plant supervisors would come into our office absolutely certain that an employee had broken work rules and needed to be punished. After listening to the supervisors, we too became convinced that punitive action was necessary. Yet, during subsequent investigations, we would discover that the details were different from what the supervisors had presented. Thus, what initially appeared to be an open and shut case wasn't so clear-cut.

I was constantly reminded that there were truly two sides to almost every story and it was wise not to give too quick of an opinion or rush to judgment. It was an invaluable experience and taught me to constantly search for the truth and not be swayed by a one-sided version that was being fed to me.

People who say "I just tell it like it is" like to pride themselves on their abilities to speak their minds and believe they have the corner on the truth market. A more accurate statement would be "I just tell it like I see it." They are simply offering their personal perspective of what they know from their own experiences and values. What they believe to be true and the actual truth might be quite different.

That is why I'm always cautious about what comes out of the mouths of political types, news commentators and radio talk-show hosts. Just one time I'd like to hear one of the famous radio talking heads say to a caller who disagrees, "Gee, I never thought about that. I was wrong." No, their livelihoods are staked to their aura of certainty. And, many listeners like that certitude – as it provides direction for their own thinking – and they believe everything that is said. It's been my experience that people want to believe in something. Right or wrong, they want to believe.

Opinion leaders and politicians often fill this void. But, I would be a little careful and stay away from the loudest of the loud. If you see or hear someone who is constantly riding a high horse, remind yourself that if he or she falls off, it's a long ways down.

We are All in This Together

It seems the older I get, the more I forget to close my zipper. There are times I wander around for several hours before I notice the gaping hole in my pants. Upon discovery, I discreetly zip up, then spend time wondering about where I've been and who might have witnessed my unknowing exhibitionism.

A few years ago, I was standing at the gate in an airport when a young man approached me and said, "Sir, I don't want to embarrass you but your zipper is open." I looked down and my zipper was not only screaming, "I'm really, really open down here!" but I was also revealing the color of my boxer shorts (blue).

Thoroughly red-faced, I thanked the young man for having the courage to tell me. And, following his lead, I have made it a point ever since to tell other people, strangers included, when they need to zip up.

It doesn't end with zippers. At a food court in a mall, I watched a guy devour a hot pizza. In his haste, he got a little careless and a foot of thin white cheese descended from his chin. Two young girls sitting at an adjacent table giggled and pointed at him. As he passed my table I said, "Young man, I don't know you so please don't be upset when I tell you this but you've got a bunch of cheese hanging from your chin." A bit taken aback, he quickly brushed off the cheese with his crumpled napkin. And he thanked me saying, "I wouldn't look too cool walking around with that on my face."

It doesn't end with food on the face, either. I was on a tour bus in New York City when Joe, our tour guide, announced that we would be stopping in front of the Empire State Building. "The police department doesn't allow us to park there for more than a minute," he said. "So, when I yell 'go' the people that want to tour it have to run off this bus in a hurry. Got it?"

We were still a few blocks away when an older guy decided he had to go to the bathroom in the back of the bus. A few minutes later we stopped in front of the Empire State Building and Joe yelled, "Go! Go! Go!"

Our companion flew out of the bathroom, grabbed his camera and ran off the bus.

Those remaining on the bus, including me, stared out the windows as he walked briskly down the busy sidewalk – with three feet of toilet paper fluttering just above the belt line of his pants. After a few seconds of disbelieving silence, those of us still on the bus broke out into hysterical laughter. Our companion later told me a woman grabbed him and gave him the bad news. He was grateful, of course.

All of us have moments where life plays one of its little jokes at our expense. Not wanting to come off as a "busy body" by sticking our nose into a place it isn't invited but having a sincere desire to look out for each other, a moment of embarrassment can give way to good-natured laughter. It's good to laugh at ourselves. And, we remember that none of us is perfect.

Take Howard's Tip about Generosity

When I joined a group of fans traveling to a college football game in California, my assigned roommate was ninety years old. Howard was a very kind and gentle soul. Sporting a gray flattop haircut, the retired college professor always wore a suit and tie – even to football games.

On the morning we checked out of our hotel room, Howard placed two one-dollar bills under the receiver of the telephone. "I always try to give a few dollars to the cleaning staff," he told me. "They don't get paid very much and they work pretty hard."

Until that moment, I had never thought about it. The housecleaning staff is usually an invisible entity at hotels. Maybe that's why most of us don't even consider leaving a tip. I'm convinced it isn't because people are cheap. Most people I know are big-hearted when they have a reason to be.

If you think about it, a guest will tip the bellman for transporting luggage bags, a valet for parking a car, a concierge for advice on things to do in the area, a waiter in the dining area and the bartender. Yet, I'd wager that the cleaning staff makes far less income than any of those positions.

I did a little research and discovered that housekeepers make minimum wage up to $14.50 an hour – the swanky places are on the high end. Housekeepers clean, on average, thirteen to fifteen rooms a day. At some places the figure jumps to thirty rooms a day. That's a lot of beds and dirty towels.

According to a study by a major university, any tips left for the cleaning staff range from one dollar to five dollars per night, depending on the quality of the hotel.

Imagine if everyone left one or two dollars for a housekeeper – or just empty their pockets of change. It could mean an extra twenty to thirty dollars a day. For those moms doing the cleaning – forty percent of mothers are the sole or primary breadwinners for their families – such small gifts, collectively, can make an enormous difference.

Ever the teacher, Howard taught me that sometimes it doesn't cost too much at all to be generous.

Something Extra:
Respect the Flag

My hometown was celebrating its centennial. As it was after midnight, most of the old folks had gone home. The main street was filled with loud young people, fueled by spirits and the energy of the night our town turned one hundred years old.

American flags hung on small flag poles that were affixed to the light posts that lined the street. A large group of people had gathered on the north end of the street so I moved in that direction. Soon, a young man reached up and yanked an American flag out of its metal holder and began waving it. Emboldened by the attention he created, he thought it would be funny to drape the flag over one of his friends – which he did.

Out of the corner of my eye I saw someone break from the crowd and move quickly toward the young man who was holding the flag. It was Herbert Pleinis. I'd known Herbert since I was a kid as I played youth baseball with his two sons. Then in his mid-sixties, Herbert was a World War II veteran where he saw the ugliness of war in the Philippines and South Pacific. He was part of what broadcaster Tom Brokaw coined as *The Greatest Generation*.

Herbert gently but firmly pulled the flag pole out of the young man's hand and in a calm but matter-of-fact voice, said, "A lot of boys died trying to protect this flag. You ought to learn to respect it."

He turned around, placed the flag back in its holder and disappeared into the crowd. I heard another young guy say, "What's *his* problem?"

Herbert didn't have a problem. To him, the flag

meant far more than bright colors and woven cloth. He saw friends die under that flag. Over the years he attended the funerals of many other military veterans whose bodies lay inside coffins which were covered by the American flag. The flag was a sacred symbol, a common bond that linked generations of patriots who put their lives on the line to protect our freedoms.

When Herbert looked at the American flag, he saw honor, duty and sacrifice.

And, he made me see it, too.

About the Author

V.J. Smith grew up with three brothers and four sisters in the small farming community of Eureka, S.D. He graduated from South Dakota State University and considers himself fortunate to have served as the Executive Director of the SDSU Alumni Association. A professional speaker for two decades, V.J. gives presentations to businesses, organizations and schools throughout the United States.

He credits his father for having instilled in him a love of public speaking. V.J. recalls, "My dad was a gifted speaker. He was an attorney by trade, but he relished the opportunities to give speeches. And, I admired the way he could communicate with his audiences."

As for his writing, V.J. was inspired by his mother. "My mom had an insatiable appetite for reading books. And, her greatest desire was to have her own book published. She sent countless manuscripts to book publishers over the years but all she ever got back were rejection letters. So, she stopped trying," V.J. said.

Thus, V.J. feels fortunate to live the dreams of both his mother and father.

Visit his website: *www.vj-smith.com*

Acknowledgments

Doug Daniel edited this book. We met in Kansas City more than thirty years ago. Doug was more than a wordsmith for this project. His advice was invaluable.

I'd also like to thank these people: Julie, Molly, Nick, Dan, Kelly, Adam, Tom, Laura, Mary Cecile, Jim, Kathryn, Terry, Tim, Laurel, Barb, Mike, Steve, Stana, Ann, Wendy, Tom, Merida, Jan, Jennifer, Geoff and JD. They are members of my immediate family and I appreciate them putting up with me.

Finally, thank you for reading this book.